Statistics for Counselors

Advanced Praise for

M000111303

Applied Statistics: Concepts for Counselors

"If you need to review basic statistics and don't know where to begin, this book is perfect! It makes difficult concepts easy to understand. I would recommend it for my undergraduate students who haven't had statistics in a while and need a refresher, or for graduate students facing their first graduate level research class!"
—Heather L. Kelly, Psy.D., Professor of Psychology, Evangel University, Springfield, Missouri, USA

"I really appreciated the places where you gave applied examples. For me, those have always helped me to understand the function of statistics."
—Nick Schollars, M.S., Mental Health Counseling

"This comprehensive yet concise overview of statistical concepts related to counseling research and practice, is a much needed *must-read* for all counselling graduate students before they start writing their research proposal. Too often I've had to read research proposals where candidates have just not done the necessary legwork before deciding on what and why they want to research the topic, and **how** they want to do it. This text would be an important starting point - once they have decided, much more detail (not included in this text) would have to be explored, but this primer will help graduates find their way in making those important research decisions at the start of their journey. They will thank Geoff Sutton for helping them find their way and pointing them in the right direction."
—Dr Mervin Van der Spuy, Psychopharmacologist & Couples Therapist, Paraklesis Counselling, Calgary, Alberta, Canada

APPLIED STATISTICS

CONCEPTS FOR COUNSELORS

Geoffrey W. Sutton, Ph.D.

Sunflower Press

APPLIED STATISTICS

CONCEPTS FOR COUNSELORS

To past and present friends among the Counseling and Psychology faculty and students of Evangel University and AGTS

APPLIED STATISTICS

CONCEPTS FOR COUNSELORS

Table of Contents

Introduction

I wrote this book to help graduate students and counselors review statistical concepts related to counseling research and practice. I have included a wide selection of statistical concepts common to courses on statistics and research methods. In this book, you will find an explanation of core statistical concepts with examples from counseling practice and research. I have not included many formulas because most spreadsheets and statistical software programs calculate the basic statistics presented in this book. This book should be helpful to the following people.

1. Graduate students in Counseling. If you are planning to attend a graduate Counselor Preparation program, this book can help you review the statistical concepts you learned as an undergraduate.

2. Students studying statistics. If you are taking, or about to take, a graduate course in testing, assessment, research methods, or statistics, this book provides an easy-to-read overview of the common statistical concepts covered in such courses

3. Counselors. If you are a counselor, you may wish to review statistical concepts to better understand test reports, conference presentations, or research articles.

4. Students taking an exam. If you need to review statistics related to a major test or exam, you might find this book helpful.

5. Researchers. If you would like to work with a researcher, this book can help you refresh your memory about statistical concepts before collaborating on a project.

6. Professors. If you are looking for a book to help students who struggle with statistics, this concise conceptual guide may help. You will see in the reviews that other professors think this book meets that need.

7. Others. Although my focus is on counseling, reviewers suggested this book would be useful for undergraduate and first year graduate students in psychology.

This book is not designed to provide readers with the detail normally found in a one semester course in statistics. I have not included the formulas to calculate most statistics and I have not provided an in-depth discussion of probability. In addition, this is not a book about research design. I have referred to basic designs from the perspective of statistical techniques used in the analysis of data. For example, I refer to two-group and multigroup designs when presenting t tests and ANOVA. This book is not a replacement for courses on assessment, but I did include a section on common test scores as well as reliability and validity associated with assessment.

I hope you will find this book a useful review.

Geoffrey W. Sutton

Springfield, Missouri, USA

Unit 1: Overview

Statistics in Perspective

1. Counselors and Science

How do scientists study counseling?

Objective:

> Identify common components of the scientific process.

When people seek assistance from a counselor, they present information in a variety of ways. They usually complete intake forms, answer interview questions, report their interests and concerns with words, display nonverbal behavior, and complete assessment questionnaires. Some of the data are numerical such as age and a score on a test. Other data may be counted such as the frequency of positive statements communicated to a romantic partner or the number of times in a day a student experiences test anxiety. Some data help us better understand an individual and the extent of their concerns. Some data help us understand people in comparison to groups of people who have taken tests of intelligence, achievement, mood, or personality. Other data may be added to a database and help us understand more about people who share similar interests or concerns. Finally, some data can help us evaluate how well a program is working such as an after-school program or premarital counseling group.

When we systematically collect data from clients, we use an empirical approach to the study of human behavior. The data may be words, which we collect as text. And as noted above, other data may be numerical, which can be analyzed in various ways depending on our goals. In this book, I am only describing numerical data and how we can use statistics to analyze those data.

Scientific Method

Counselors and counselor educators may focus their careers on counseling research. When they use an empirical approach to collect data, they will follow some rules, which scientists have found useful for decades. Different authors describe the steps in slightly different ways. Here is a seven-part process that captures the common parts of the research process and illustrates where data and statistics fit in the process. Following are the seven components

Identify a Problem or Topic

Researchers begin with a topic of interest often referred to as *a problem to be solved*. Often, they formulate the problem in question format. Here are some examples

- What percentage of graduates from a substance abuse treatment program remain sober after one year?
- How effective is the new medication for the treatment of depression?
- What counseling techniques help most people decrease aggressive behavior?
- What counselor characteristics are relevant to developing rapport?

Researchers review articles published in professional journals to learn what other scientists have discovered before planning their own study. By considering what has been done, researchers are in a better position to avoid past mistakes and consider new questions that need to be answered.

State Hypotheses

Following the formulation of general questions, researchers state their hypotheses. Most studies include several hypotheses, which are statements of expectations based on previous research or a theory. For example, if a new approach to couples' counseling was useful in a university study, a counseling researcher might hypothesize that it would be effective in a community sample. A school counselor might hypothesize that a peer network in a local school might help reduce bullying.

Create Designs

Research designs are plans. They are ways of organizing a study so that we can have confidence that the data we collect really answers the questions we formed. A design identifies who will be in a study, where it will be done, how we will collect data and any other procedures necessary to ensure that the data are trustworthy.

Collect Data

When all procedures are in place, the research team begins the process of collecting data. People may answer survey questions online or answer questions at the end of a counseling session or program. Some people may take formal tests, which produce a set of scores. Data can be obtained by observers. Observing behavior can be done in several ways. Here are a few examples:

- Observing playground behavior for evidence of bullying
- Observing recordings of couple interactions for evidence of empathic listening

- Observing counseling sessions for active listening skills

Analyze Data

Once the data have been collected, they are usually organized into a database. Researchers then use software to calculate a variety of statistics designed to describe the people in the study and answer the questions posed at the beginning of the study.

Interpret Results

The results of statistical calculations can be interpreted in different ways. Complex analyses can be difficult to interpret. Researchers may focus on a particular finding and inadvertently miss other analyses, that contradict a particular conclusion. Consider a simple example. A counselor may avoid an intervention that routinely fails with 30% of people. But what if we focused on the 70% who usually benefit from the intervention?

Disseminate Results

The final part of the research process is dissemination. Researchers make their findings public, usually in the form of a journal article or presentation at a professional conference. This public dissemination is vital to a scientific approach to counseling because others have the opportunity to ask questions about the research methods and how the results were interpreted. In this way, science is self-correcting.

The acronym is PHD CARD. I realize it is a bit cheesy but I hope it helps you think of researchers who may have a PHD on their virtual business CARD. Here's the list again.

P   Identify a problem or topic

H   State hypotheses

D   Design a study

C   Collect data

A   Analyze the data

R   Interpret the results of the analysis

D   Disseminate the results

Terms for Numbers and Data

Most of the examples in this book refer to quantitative data. Quantitative data are numbers. Numbers may be test scores or values. The broad term for a number in a data set is a *value*. Values that result from scoring a test, quiz, or survey are called *scores*. Other numerical values that are not scores include age, height, weight, and rankings. Researchers commonly refer to a group of data as a *data set*. All the numbers in a data set are values. Some of the values are scores on tests and quizzes and some are not.

Data sets are usually in the form of spreadsheets where each row represents a person such as a client or research participant. The columns contain data about the person. The data are usually either text or numbers.

Technically speaking, *data* is a plural noun and takes a plural verb so we write data *are* and not data *is*. We refer to *these* data not *this* data. The singular form of *data* is *datum*, which is rarely used. *Datum* is the term for one score or one value but you will rarely see the word *datum*. In general writing, you will see people do not treat *data* as a plural noun but in scientific writing and presentations, treat *data* as a plural noun.

Review

What are common steps in the research process?

What are some examples of data that a counselor might encounter in a counseling practice?

What are some types of tests that would produce numerical scores?

2. Counseling Research

What do counselors study?

Objective:

Describe four types of counseling research.

Counseling research can take many directions. In this chapter I will illustrate a few examples so you have a context for the contribution of statistics to the research process.

When clients seek counseling they present facts about themselves during the initial interview. In addition, some take tests that produce scores. If a client has one or more mental health conditions, a counselor may assign a diagnosis and assess severity using a numerical system. All of these data can be accumulated by counselors. Counseling researchers may collect data from many counselors and study characteristics of people in large databases. Here are some examples of information that could come from a large database of people who seek counseling.

- Percentage of people having various characteristics, who begin and complete counseling
- Average client age
- Percentage of people with different ethnic backgrounds
- Percentage of people from different socioeconomic backgrounds
- Percentage of people having different religious or spiritual interests

In addition to the basic descriptive values listed above, we might also discover the percentage of people requesting help with the following:

- Communication difficulties
- Career planning
- Parenting strategies
- Coping with depression, anxiety, or other mental health concerns
- Relationship difficulties

Researchers can study aspects of the counseling process itself. Researchers are interested in the effectiveness of different counseling approaches such as cognitive-behavioral therapy and gestalt strategies. Others are interested in the relative value of individual versus group interventions. Counseling researchers may also study treatment formats such as a 20 to 25-minute weekly session, a 45 to 50-minute session, or an intensive intervention lasting a weekend or most of a week. In addition to personal information, researchers collect data to demonstrate effectiveness and satisfaction. Statistical analyses can help identify the most effective and most satisfying dimension of counseling for different participants.

A third type of research has to do with counselor assessment instruments. Most people have had the experience of taking tests of achievement in school. Many have taken tests that help explore attitudes, personality, values, and vocational interests. These tests produce scores that can be analyzed to help the test taker and the counselor understand a person's standing compared to others in a reference group. A reference group might be other students or employees. In addition to descriptive information, some tests can be used in conjunction with other data to predict success in college or in an employment setting.

Our final example of research is program evaluation. Counseling researchers are interested in learning how well programs help. Researchers can collect data to evaluate several aspects of a program including how well the program works as a whole as well as the success of the process and various components within the program. Some examples of programs include the following:

- After school programs for children
- Parenting programs conducted at various community sites or "take-home" programs that use video and text presentations
- Substance abuse and dependence programs
- Career exploration programs
- Intensive weekend marriage programs
- Sex-education program in a school
- Forgiveness workshop

There are other types of research completed by counselors and scientists in other professions. Almost any study of how people think, feel, and act could be linked to the work of a counselor. Counselors learn about people and their needs by contributing to the formation of a local or national database, studying various components of counseling, evaluating tests and other assessment tools and conducting program evaluations.

Review

Identify and give examples of four types of counseling research presented in the chapter.

What are additional data you might include in a client database?

What are additional components of the counseling process you could study?

What tests are you familiar with?

What are some additional programs of interest to a counselor?

3. Variables

How are people alike or different?

Objectives:

Define *variable*.

Describe different types of variables.

Define *independent* and *dependent* variables.

We describe ourselves and others in many ways. We often make comparisons that suggest people can vary on a particular trait or characteristic. We quickly notice obvious things like gender presentation and colors of skin, hair, eyes, and clothes. We especially notice differences that contrast with people we see in our daily life. Counselors are interested in those similarities and differences relevant to helping people achieve their counseling goals. For example, we may recognize a client's symptoms of depression as similar to others', but the symptoms may vary in severity and how long they have persisted. People are different. They have characteristics that vary from one person to another.

In counseling research, variables are characteristics or events that vary in two or more ways. In contrast, a constant is a characteristic that does not vary. Researchers attempt to "hold" characteristics or events constant if they might interfere with interpreting the results of a counseling intervention. For example, we may "hold counselor constant" by having only one counselor provide services during a study or we may "hold counseling constant" by having all counselors use the same procedures during couple's counseling. Other examples of constants can include appointment times, counselor clothing, counseling rooms, and facilities that are the same or similar in important respects. Beyond the observable characteristics like color of hair and eyes, we describe people in terms of happiness, anger, hopefulness, extroversion, and so forth. Most of the time, we describe people in terms of unseen characteristics. Sometimes we use simple categories like *hopeful* and *hopeless*. At other times, we think in terms of a range of values. For example, we may describe level of hope using words such as *very low* or *very high*.

In 1991, C.R. Snyder and his colleagues published research on a measure of hope known as the *Dispositional Hope Scale*. The items on the scale could be rated from 1 (*definitely false*) to 8 (*definitely true*). The ratings on each item can be added to yield a total score for hope. Thus, to be more precise, we may assign numerical values to unseen constructs like hope. The construct of hope is a measurable variable. The spread of scores on a hope scale can help researchers describe the range of hope in individuals or groups of people.

Variables may be categorical or continuous. Categorical variables may have multiple categories in a worldwide population but in a study, a researcher may choose to examine only two categories. For example, there are many grades in school, but researchers may decide to compare students in Grades 4 and 5. In this example, grade is a variable varied in two ways—two categories of students. Other categorical variables include ethnicity, sex, religious affiliation, relationship status, and military status.

Continuous variables are those variables having a wide range of numerical values. Examples of continuous variables include age, intelligence, achievement, and personality traits such as agreeableness, extroversion, and conscientiousness. Mental health concerns are also measured on scales yielding a range of values for depression, anxiety, and anger.

Variables in Research

In descriptive research, statistics are used to describe how people score on the variables of interest in the study. For example, a researcher could administer a personality test containing five personality traits. Each trait is a variable. The researcher could also look at patterns to see how people are similar or different on all of the traits in the study.

When researchers want to discover what might help people increase their self-esteem or capacity to cope with trauma, the researchers are looking for cause and effect relationships among the variables. In this type of research, variables are identified as *independent* and *dependent*. Independent variables are those thought to produce a change or effect in another variable called the *dependent variable*. Dependent variables are those variables expected to change when the researchers vary the level of the independent variable. Researchers use the letters *IV* and *DV* to identify independent and dependent variables. In a simple study, researchers may identify a new treatment program to reduce alcohol abuse. The alcohol abuse treatment program can be an IV if we vary it in at least two ways. A simple variation is to present people with either the new or the old treatment programs. After the programs are delivered, the effects of treatment can be measured on one or more dependent variables, or DVs, such as measures of alcohol use and craving for alcohol.

Another common variable type is an extraneous variable (EV), also called a *confounding variable* or *CV*. It is not always possible to measure CVs, but when they can be measured, researchers can determine if the CV is related to the DV. For example, researchers could study the relationship of years of education to alcohol abuse. If education makes a difference, then an alcohol treatment program alone would not be the only variable causing changes in alcohol abuse.

It can be difficult to identify variables in an article unless we focus on the function of a variable in the study. Gratitude can be an independent, dependent, or confounding variable in research. Robert Emmons is probably the world's leading expert on gratitude. Increasing gratitude has many benefits. We could offer a gratitude program at a counseling center. If we varied the program such that some people get gratitude education and some keep a gratitude journal without attending presentations, then the type of gratitude program functions as an independent variable. If we include a gratitude questionnaire as part of a gratitude program evaluation, then gratitude functions as a dependent variable, which is measured by the gratitude questionnaire. Finally, gratitude can be a confounding variable. Suppose counselors conduct a forgiveness workshop and use questionnaires as part of their workshop program evaluation plan. If they fail to measure gratitude, then their interpretation of the data may be confounded because gratitude influences forgiveness. According to Emmons, people with higher levels of gratitude are more forgiving than those with lower levels of gratitude. You can learn more about Emmons' research, at this link. https://greatergood.berkeley.edu/profile/Robert_Emmons

Review

In counseling research, variables are characteristics that vary in two or more ways.

Categorical variables may have multiple categories in a worldwide population but in a study, a researcher may choose to examine only two categories.

Continuous variables are those variables having a wide range of numerical values.

Variables may also be classified as independent, dependent, and extraneous or confounding.

4. Forming Groups

What is sampling?

Objectives:

Define *sample* and *population*.

Describe different types of samples.

Define and give an example of *sample bias*.

Sampling is a research method that allows scientists to study characteristics of people or other entities by looking at the characteristics of a small subset of the larger group. The subset is a *sample* taken from the larger group, which is the *population*. Populations consist of all members of a group as defined by the researcher's interest. Examples of populations include all counselors in the United States, all school counselors in elementary schools, and all clients at a counseling center. A sample is a small group drawn in a specific way from the population. Samples may be further subdivided into smaller groups.

The numbers or values that describe the population are called *parameters* and those that describe the sample are called *statistics*. When writing about the values scientists use Greek letters for population values and italicized letters from our alphabet for statistical values. Here are two examples. We will review the meaning of these terms in a later chapter.

Population	Sample	Term
μ	*M*	Mean or arithmetic average
σ	*SD*	Standard Deviation

Sample bias

Not all samples are the same. If we take a sample of 20 counselors from a population of 1,000, our small sample may contain counselors that do not share important characteristics typical of those in the population. For example, the counselors in our sample might have more or less empathy than those in the population. When sample statistics are very different from the population values, we refer to the sample as *biased*. This is an important concern for researchers. Here are some examples of biased samples in counseling research.

- A professor studies beliefs about marijuana use expressed by a sample of students attending a large state university. Such students might have different beliefs than students in religious schools or smaller schools.
- A counselor studies the effectiveness of a parenting program in a sample of mothers but does not include fathers.
- A graduate student conducts a study on the internet by posting links on social networking sites and sending emails to people on available lists.
- A client forms an opinion about counseling and counselors in general based on experience with two counselors.

In each of the above cases, the sampling method introduces an unknown. The professor cannot assume all students share the same beliefs about marijuana. There may be some characteristic of students at religious schools or smaller schools that accounts for differences in beliefs about marijuana. It could be that a parenting program that works well for mothers will also work well for fathers but we will not know that until we study the program in a sample of fathers. The graduate student has attempted to get a large sample, yet many people do not have internet access and do not participate in social networking sites. Others do not have email or do not check their accounts on a regular basis. Finally, clients, like other people, often form opinions about methods and professions based on their experience. Our experiences are usually limited to a small sample of all possible experiences.

Sampling Methods

Convenience sample

Professors, graduate students, and counselors in practice often use *convenience samples* composed of people who are available and willing to participate in a study. We often do not know the characteristics of those who refuse to participate. *Volunteer bias* or *self-selection bias*, is a known problem. Researchers have learned that volunteers tend to be better educated and have a higher socio-economic status than those who do not volunteer.

Random sample

If you want to study the satisfaction of clients at your center, you could take a *random sample* from the full list of persons. If every person selected agrees to participate, you have an *unbiased sample*. This rarely happens so there will be some error in sampling due to the lack of full participation. Researchers correct for *sampling error* using statistical procedures. You may have seen the results of news polls that report a percentage of people who will likely vote for a political candidate as 55% plus or minus 2%. The plus-or-minus values indicate a range of values to accommodate an estimated error in the sample.

Although we can use the data from biased samples, we must use caution in interpreting the results and be careful to acknowledge the error or bias in the sample.

Review

How is a sample related to a population?

Describe the types of samples presented in the chapter.

Provide examples of biased samples.

5. Measurement

What kind of number is that?

Objective:

Describe four types of measurement.

Before calculating statistics, we need to know what the numbers mean. We use numbers in different ways. In this chapter we will look at four ways researchers use numbers. These four concepts are known as *scales of measurement* or *levels of measurement* and include: nominal, ordinal, interval, and ratio scales (or levels). I will use the word *scale* for each concept.

Nominal scale

The nominal scale is a naming scale. We can refer to groups with names. When we use numbers, the numbers just refer to categories, and higher numbers do not mean more of an item or a particular order. Sometimes numbers are used like codes to identify people. Here are some examples:

- People identified by sex-linked gender where 1 = woman and 2 = man
- Sports uniforms with numbers used to identify different players
- Ethnic groups labeled by perceived continent of origin such as Asian or African
- Employment status, such as employed, unemployed, retired, and so forth

Ordinal scale

A second scale is the ordinal scale. As the name implies, order matters. People rank themselves or others on a characteristic from high to low. The quantitative difference between Ranks 1 and 2 and the ranks 2 and 3 could be very different. The ordinal scale does not recognize the size of these differences. It only recognizes the rank order. Here are some rankings related to counseling:

- After listing your job preferences, order the top five from most to least favorite.
- Considering your depression in the past month, on a scale from 1 to 10, how would you rate your depression today if 10 is the worst it has ever been?
- List your current courses and rank them from high to low based on your interest level.
- Look at these five conference proposals and rank them from 1 to 5 where 5 represents your top-rated proposal.

Interval scale

The third measurement scale is the interval scale. The difference between values on an interval scale are considered equal. Although scientists sometimes debate the merits of the equality of the intervals, common examples of such scales in counseling may include the following:

- A test that measures intelligence
- A test that measures academic achievement, such as in reading or math
- A test that organizes answers into scores for various dimensions of personality.
- A test that measures several dimensions of healthy relationships.

Ratio scale

Finally, the ratio scale, like the interval scale, has equal intervals, but unlike the interval scale, the ratio scale has a true zero point. Examples of ratio scales include tape measures and scales that measure weight. In the cases of height and weight, it is reasonable to refer to ratios. For example, a person weighing 300 pounds is twice as heavy as a person who weighs 150 pounds. In contrast, it is not reasonable to think of a person with an IQ (intelligence quotient) of 140 (interval scale) as having twice the intelligence of a person with an IQ of 70.

Review

Four common types of measurement include nominal, ordinal, interval, and ratio scales.

Look at the examples for each measurement type to help recognize the type of measurement reported in test manuals and research reports.

Try to think of additional examples for each type of measurement.

Unit 2: Describing Groups of Clients and Participants

6. Frequencies and Percentages

How often? What percentage?

Objectives:

Define *frequency*.

Define *percentage*.

How frequently do couples argue about finances, have sex, or complain about sharing responsibilities? What percentage of people experienced depression last year? What percentage of counseling students find employment within a year following graduation? Data presented as frequencies and percentages are fairly easy to understand. In this chapter, I will review the basic concepts. Also, because the calculations are fairly easy, I will show you how to obtain the answers to basic questions.

Frequencies

A frequency is the number of people in a sample who have a specific score. If 25 students obtained a score of 100 on a reading test, then we would write $f = 25$ for a score of 100. Researchers use the letter n for the number of people and often use the letter X for a score. The letters are in italics. The f for frequency is lower case, and the n is lower case for a sample or portion of a sample. Use an upper-case N when referring to all of the people in a set of data or a population.

Percentages

According to the U.S. National Center for Education Statistics (NCES; May, 2016), 13% of students enrolled in public school during 2013-2014 were identified as having a learning disability. Use the percent symbol (%) when reporting percentages. If you found that 15% of people experienced depression in the past year, you would know that for any representative sample of 100 people, 15 of them would have experienced depression in the past year. You calculate percentage by dividing the number of people with depression by the number of people in your sample and multiplying the result by 100.

Let's take another example. Suppose you wish to know how many students in a small college have a learning disability. First, you analyze data from last year and find that of 1,000 students, 130 have a learning disability. So far you know $N = 1000$ for the total number of students and $n = 130$ for the group that reported a learning disability. If you divide 130 by 1000 and multiple by 100 you find 13% have a learning disability ($130 \div 1000 \times 100 = 13\%$).

Frequencies, Percentages, and Categories

Spirituality is an important aspect of life for many people. Researchers at pewforum.org looked at the frequency of prayer practiced by people from different faiths. One chart presents the percentage of people praying at different frequency levels. For example, 55% pray daily and 16% pray weekly.

They also presented a chart that combined frequencies, percentages, and religious groups. Following are a few examples:

- 43% of Buddhists pray at least daily and 20% weekly
- 59% of Catholics pray at least daily and 20% weekly
- 69% or Muslims pray at least daily and 9% weekly

Review

A frequency is the number of people in a sample who have a specific score.

Calculate the percentage of people with a characteristic by dividing the number of people with the characteristic by the number of people in the sample and multiplying the result by 100.

Counselors are interested in the frequency of a characteristic in a population and the percentage of people having that characteristic. Provide examples of personal characteristics a counselor might like to study.

Here's the link to the pewforum chart mentioned above. http://www.pewforum.org/religious-landscape-study/frequency-of-prayer/

7. Distribution of Data

How can we visualize data?

Objectives:

Describe a frequency polygon.

Describe a histogram.

If counselors were to administer a reading test to a random sample of 244 adults, they would find that some people have very high reading skills and that some have very low reading skills but most people fall in a middle range of scores. Scores from this fictitious sample are included in the table below, which is known as a *frequency distribution* of data. In this example, the data are scores represented by the upper case and italicized letter X.

Distribution of Reading Scores (N = 244).

X	f
36	1
38	4
40	8
42	12
44	16
46	26
48	35
50	40
52	35
54	26
56	16
58	12
60	8
62	4
64	1

Recall that the frequency (*f*) column represents how many people obtained the score in the *X* column. When we plot the frequencies on a graph, we obtain a frequency polygon as shown in the following chart.

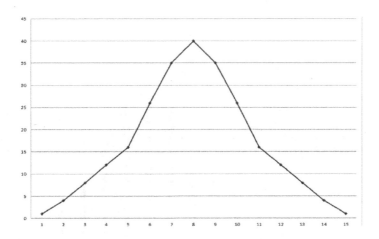

Frequency polygon for the reading scores in the preceding table.

If we were to plot the data from a larger sample, the lines connecting the points in the polygon would smooth into a curve known as the *normal curve* or *bell curve*. The normal curve shape of a large distribution of scores is a common finding for scores on many tests such as tests that measure intelligence, memory, academic achievement, personality traits, and language skills. We will learn more about this curve in future chapters. For now, notice that most scores are in the middle with very few on either the left or the right. Also, notice that the shape is symmetrical. The *x*-axis is the horizontal axis and the *y*-axis is the vertical axis.

Another common chart is the histogram. In this chart, the numbers on the x-axis are the reading scores, and the height of each bar (y-axis) represents the frequency of each score.

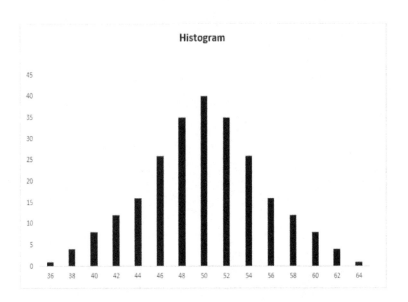

Review

In counseling, data are often scores on a test but data can also be numbers representing age or grade.

In statistics, an upper case and italicized letter X is often used for scores from one test or data set. A lower case italicized f represents frequency.

How can we create a frequency polygon from a frequency table of scores?

What do the x-and y-axes of a histogram represent when creating a chart for the frequency of a set of scores?

8. On Average

What is an average?

Objectives:

Define and calculate a *mode*.

Define and calculate a *median*.

Define and calculate a *mean*.

Referring to averages is a short-hand way of describing what is typical about a set of data. Statisticians use the more precise phrase *central tendency* to refer to values typical of the center of a set of scores or other data values. There are three common measures of central tendency: the mode, the median, and the mean.

Mode

The mode is the most frequent score. The symbol for the mode is *Mo*. Suppose five clients earn the following scores on a forgiveness scale: [10, 11, 12, 14, 11]. The most frequent score is 11, so the mode = 11. The modal value can vary more than the median and the mean so it is often ignored or only reported along with the median or mean, which are more stable. In this context, the phrase *more stable* means a value is less likely to be different in another sample.

Median

The median is the middle value in a set of data. The symbol for the median is *Mdn*. Because the median is the middle value, it is the 50th percentile. The median cuts a set of scores in half so that half the scores are above and half are below the median. To find the median, arrange a set of scores in order from low to high then choose the middle number. For example, suppose seven students earn the following scores on a spelling test [21, 22, 10, 17, 21, 19, 14]. First, place the scores in order from low to high as follows: [10, 14, 17, 19, 21, 21, 22]. Next, find the middle value, which would be the fourth value. Thus, the median = 19. There are three scores above and three below the median.

Here's a trickier situation. Suppose eight clients complete the following numbers of assigned tasks after five counseling sessions: [7, 11, 13, 13, 15, 16, 16, 16]. The median for this set is 14, but 14 does not appear in the data set. We use the number 14 because it is midway between the two middle values of 13 and 15. As you can see, four numbers are above and four are below the number 14. When there is an even number of scores, the median is the average of the two middle scores. You can simply add 13 and 15 to get 28, then divide 28 by 2 to get 14. When there is an odd number of scores in a data set, then the median is the middle score.

Mean

The mean is the arithmetic average value for a set of data. The symbol for the mean is M. To obtain the average, you add all of the scores and divide their sum by the number of scores. For example, five clients in treatment for anxiety obtain the following scores on an anxiety scale [18, 21, 22, 23, 16]. When we add the five scores, they total 100. If we divide 100 by the number of scores, which is 5, we obtain a value of 20. The mean of the set of scores is 20. Let me illustrate this another way. First add the scores: $18+21+22+23+16 = 100$. Then divide the sum of the scores (100) by the number of scores (5) to find the average score of 20. Notice that none of the clients obtained a score of 20. The number 20 represents an average anxiety score for a group of clients. Because the mean requires us to average every score in a set of data, it is more sensitive to all the values in a data set than either the mode or the median, which only consider the most frequent or middle values.

When a set of scores includes one or more values that are very different from most scores, the mean is not the best value to use. Scores or values that are very different from most scores or values are called *outliers*. Outliers keep us from understanding what is typical of a set of data. For example, suppose we want to know the typical age of counseling students in a graduate program. We learn that the mean age is 36 but that most counselors are below age 30. The data set contains the following ages: [28, 29, 26, 27, 70]. In this case, the median of 28 is a better measure of central tendency than the mean because the median is less affected by extreme scores.

Sample error

It is important to keep in mind that a calculation of the mean for a sample only estimates the mean of the population if the sample truly represents the population in all important respects. We often do not know the population mean so we ought to be cautious in making assumptions about our findings. Statistics programs will estimate the *Standard Error of the Mean*, abbreviated as SE or *se*. I will discuss the *Standard Error of the Mean* later after reviewing the properties of a normal distribution.

Review

Define *mode, median,* and *mean.*

Based on the text, what is an *outlier*?

Based on the text, which measure of central tendency is most likely distorted by an extreme value?

Provide the commonly used abbreviations for *mode, median,* and *mean.*

Practice calculating the mode, median, and mean for the data in each section of this chapter.

9. Ranges

So where are the scores?

Objectives:

> Define *range*.

> Define *standard deviation*.

> Define *variance*.

Knowing an average score or value in a data set can be helpful but one number representing a central value does not tell us much about the rest of the values. In this chapter, I will discuss another statistic that describes how values are dispersed, or spread out, in a data set. Statisticians refer to these statistics as *measures of dispersion*.

Range

The range is the difference between the highest and lowest value in a set of data. Suppose we have measured forgiveness for five clients who obtain the following scores: [12, 13, 16, 15, 14]. We find that $M = 14$ and $Mdn = 14$. In this case, the range = 4, that is, $16 - 12 = 4$. The range provides a general idea of the spread of scores in a data set. However, suppose we change one score so that instead of 16, one client scored 21. Now $M = 15$ and $Mdn = 14$, but the range is $21 - 12 = 9$. One score can make a major difference in the range; thus, we can say the range statistic is not very stable.

Restriction of range can be a problem evident by a small value for the range compared to possible values if the values or scores were more spread out. In a graduate counseling program that admits only highly motivated students who had high undergraduate GPAs, the range of graduate GPAs might be very small reflecting the fact that most graduate students earn high grades for their coursework. Some statistics programs and reports refer to the highest value as *Max* for *maximum value* and the lowest value as *Min* for *minimum value*.

Standard Deviation

A more common statistic to describe a set of scores or data is the standard deviation, symbolized by a lower-case and italicized *s* in statistics books and upper case italicized *SD* in reports or tables. The standard deviation is often confusing to students when they first encounter the concept, so consider reading this section more than once.

Essentially, the standard deviation tells us an average deviation for the scores or numerical values in a data set. The standard deviation considers the average difference between each score and the mean. Getting the average deviation requires a work around strategy because the mean is the average value for a set of data. If you try to find the average difference in scores above and below the mean you will find they add up to zero, which isn't very useful.

Consider this simple example. Five child clients are ages 8, 9, 10, 11, and 12. The average or mean age is 10. Two ages are below 10, and two ages are above 10. Look at the following table of ages.

Age	M - Age
8	$10 - 8 = 2$
9	$10 - 9 = 1$
10	$10 - 10 = 0$
11	$10 - 11 = -1$
12	$10 - 12 = -2$

If you add the differences ($M -$ Age), you will find they equal zero. The negative numbers cancel the positive numbers, leaving us with zero. In numbers, $2 + 1 + 0 + (-1) + (-2) = 0$.

Statisticians solve the problem of a zero result by squaring the differences, adding the squared values, then finding the average of the squared values. The result of this procedure is called the *variance*. But the variance is based on squared values. To return to the original spread of values that are not squared, we need to take the square root of the variance. The standard deviation is the square root of the variance. The variance is the mean of the squared deviations of each data value from the mean. Sometimes the variance is called the *Mean Square* and abbreviated *MS*.

Here's how we calculate the variance (VAR) and Standard Deviation (SD) for our small data set.

First, we square the deviation values. Recall that the deviation values are the values that result when we subtract each value from the mean as illustrated in the *M*-Age column above. Also recall that the squared value of a negative number yields a positive number. The squared deviations are as follows: 4, 1, 0, 1, 4.

Second, we add the squared values: $4 + 1 + 0 + 1 + 4 = 10$. The number 10 is known as the *Sum of Squares* and abbreviated *SS*.

To find the average or mean square, we divide the 10 by the number of values in the data set, which is 5. In this example, 10 divided by 5 equals 2. The variance is 2.

The standard deviation is the square root of the variance. The square root of $2 = 1.41$ so for these data, the *SD* is 1.41.

In research papers and test results, it is common to report the mean and standard deviation. For example, a set of achievement scores for a school may be reported as $M = 100$, $SD = 15$. For our data, we would report $M = 10$, $SD = 1.41$.

Research note

In research, scientists have found that statistics based on samples may not be accurate estimates of the population. To adjust for this finding, the sample variance is found by dividing by $n - 1$ instead of n. In our simple example, the variance would be 2.5 instead of 2 because the mean of 10 divided by 4 $(n - 1) = 2.5$. The square root of 2.5 is 1.58 thus, $SD = 1.58$.

Review

The range is a simple way to describe the spread of data.

Find the range by subtracting the lowest value from the highest value.

The standard deviation is commonly reported along with the mean in test and research reports.

The standard deviation is the square root of the variance.

Review the meaning of the terms, *Sum of Squares* and *Mean Square*.

Practice calculating the range.

Describe standard deviation.

10. Distributions Part 1

What is normal?

Objectives:

Identify the location of the mode, median, and mean on a normal distribution.

Identify the percentage of scores falling between one, two, and three standard deviations from the mean when scores are normally distributed.

Define *Standard Error of the Mean*.

When researchers plot data about many aspects of human nature, they find the pattern of scores or values closely matches the shape of a bell. The bell curve is also known as the *normal curve* or *normal distribution*. This curve has mathematical properties that allow researchers to draw conclusions about where scores are located relative to other scores. In this chapter, I will review a few basic properties of the normal curve.

The three measures of central tendency (mode, median, mean) are at the same middle point in a normal curve. The numbers representing the middle of the curve divide the curve in half. In a normal distribution, 50% of scores or values are always above the mode, median, and mean. The curve is symmetrical or the same on both sides. Therefore, 50% of the scores or values are always above, and 50% always below, the mode, median, and mean.

The *x*-axis in the normal curve indicates the mean at zero and the standard deviation units above and below the mean. The height of the curve indicates the percentage of scores in that area. You can see that a large percentage of the scores are between 1 and -1 standard deviations. The ends of the distribution are called *tails*. Extreme scores are in the tails. Consider the height of the distribution at - 2.5 or +2.5 standard deviations. At these points, the curve almost touches the *x*-axis. Only a small percentage of scores is beyond 2.5 standard deviations in either direction. Theoretically, the tails of the curve never touch the baseline. Only a small fraction of a percent of scores is beyond 3 standard deviations.

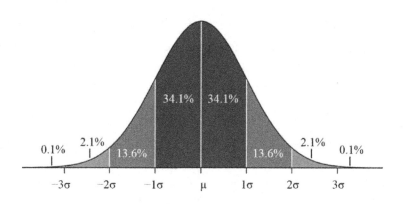

The mathematical properties of the curve help us identify where scores or values will be located when they are at standard distances from the mean. A standard distance is in standard deviation units. In counseling research, we find that most scores or values fall within three standard deviations from the mean. For example, approximately 99% of intelligence test scores will fall between -3 and +3 standard deviations from the mean.

Other common references are scores or values that are 1 and 2 standard deviations from the mean. Following are the approximate percentages of scores within three standard deviations.

68% of scores fall between + 1 and − 1 Standard Deviations from the mean.

95% of scores fall between + 2 and − 2 Standard Deviations from the mean.

99% of scores fall between + 3 and − 3 Standard Deviations from the mean.

The percentages in the above list are rounded and in common use. If we wish to be more precise, we can use two decimal points and describe the percentage of scores in each major area of the curve. Recall that the curve is symmetrical, so the percentage will be the same for each corresponding area above and below the mean.

34.13% of scores fall within 1 standard deviation from the mean.

13.59% of scores fall between 1 and 2 standard deviations from the mean.

2.15% of scores fall between 2 and 3 standard deviations from the mean.

0.13% of scores fall beyond 3 standard deviations from the mean.

Standard Error and the Mean

Now that we have reviewed the properties of a normal distribution, we can use the percentages found within one, two, and three standard deviations from the mean to talk about the standard error of the mean mentioned in the chapter about the mean.

When we calculate a mean for our samples, we should keep in mind that the mean of a different sample from the same population may vary from the mean we obtained. If we continue to take samples and calculate the mean for each sample, we will find that the means form a normal distribution. Thus, we can draw on our understanding of the normal distribution to estimate an error band around our obtained mean. Statistics programs provide us with an estimate of the standard error of the mean (SE).

Here's an example. Suppose we find that the mean score on a measure of hope is 10 for a sample of young adults. And suppose our statistics program reports an SE of 1. Given the properties of the normal curve, we can estimate that 68% of the time that we take samples from the same population our mean will fall between 9 and 11. The values 9 and 11 are obtained by subtracting one SE from our mean of 10 and adding one SE to our mean of 10. Recall that the properties of the normal curve indicate 68% of values fall within plus and minus one standard deviation from the mean of the distribution.

Now suppose you wanted to estimate where the mean on the hope measure would fall 95% of the time. This time we are considering 2 SEs. Given an SE of 1 we would expect our mean to fall between 8 and 12. Thus, we add 2 to 10 to obtain the upper range of 12, and we subtract 2 from 10 to get the lower range of 8. The 95% level is a common level to report as a degree of confidence for many statistics. In writing, you may see the statistic referred to as the 95% *confidence level*. The upper and lower values within which the mean may be located are a *confidence interval* abbreviated as *CI*.

Review

Many human characteristics conform to a normal or bell-shaped distribution.

In a normal distribution, the mode, median, and mean all fall at the same location in the middle of the distribution.

When characteristics are normally distributed, we can know what percentage of people with those characteristics fall within one, two, and three standard deviations from average.

When researchers take many samples from a population, the means of the samples will be different. The differences represent sampling error, which is normally distributed.

Because sampling error is normally distributed, it is possible to estimate where the mean will fall if another sample is taken from the same population.

Researchers often estimate the confidence interval for the mean using a 95% confidence level.

11. Distributions Part 2

What is NOT normal?

Objectives:

Define *positive* and *negative skew*.

Define *positive* and *negative kurtosis*.

In the previous chapter, we learned about the normal curve. In reality, distributions of test scores and other data do not precisely match the normal curve, which means we will need to be cautious in how we interpret findings and use tests based on the assumption our data are normally distributed. Statisticians have developed guidelines to address the problem of nonnormal distributions of data. To understand these limits, we will need to review two concepts: *skew* and *kurtosis*.

Skew

Data may be skewed in a positive or negative direction. If a lot of people earn low scores on a test, then the distribution will be positively skewed. That is, the area on the right side of the curve will be low, representing a small percentage of high scores. Recall that the positive numbers are to the right of the distribution. A difficult test is positively skewed.

If a lot of people earn high scores on a test, then the distribution will be negatively skewed. That is, the area on the left side of the curve will be low, representing a small percentage of low scores. Recall that the negative numbers are to the left of the distribution. An easy test is negatively skewed.

Statistics programs calculate skew. Statisticians vary in how much skew is permissible, so check with your professors about what limits they prefer. A common guideline is to accept values up to plus or minus 1.5.

Researchers pay attention to skew because the measures of central tendency (mean, median, mode) are no longer the same values. Recall that the mean is the most sensitive to outliers. Consider the extreme scores for positive and negative skew. Those extreme scores will result in a mean that does not represent most of the data.

In positively skewed distributions, the mean is pulled toward the right, but the mode, represented by the high point of the distribution, is to the left of the mean. The median is between the mode and the mean. On the graph, the left-to-right order for positive skew is mode, median, mean.

I created an example of positive skew.

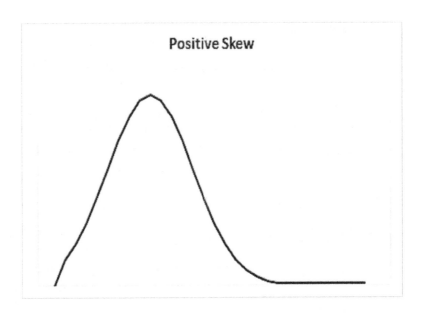

Positive Skew

In negatively skewed distributions, the mean is pulled toward the left, but the mode, represented by the high point of the distribution, is to the right of the mean. The median is between the mode and the mean. The left-to-right order for negative skew is mean, median, mode.

Following is an example of negative skew.

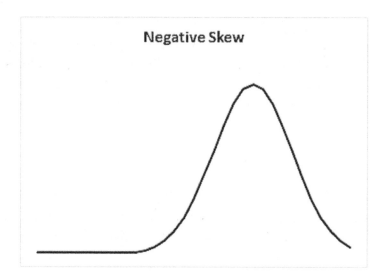

Negative Skew

Recall that statisticians call the ends of the distribution *tails*. A common phrase to talk about naming skew is "the tail tells the tale." That is, the longer tail of the distribution helps identify it as having positive or negative skew. Recall that positive numbers are on the right side and negative numbers are on the left side of a distribution.

A common example of skew and distortion of the mean can be found in salary reports. Suppose counselors earn $60,000 a year in a university counseling center where the president earns $1,000,000 and a popular coach earns $3,000,000. The few very high salaries will result in a high average salary if we use the mean. In the case of salaries, the median is usually the more accurate average to report.

Kurtosis

Researchers pay more attention to skew than they do to kurtosis. In case you encounter the term, here is a brief explanation. Some distributions have a lot of scores close to the middle, resulting in a narrowing of the mid-section of the bell in the bell curve. These distributions are called *leptokurtic*. In contrast, some distributions have a lot of similar scores which are plotted as a flatter distribution called *platykurtic*. Like the values for skew, statisticians use a range of plus and minus 1.5 for an acceptable range of kurtosis.

Other variations

Distributions can vary in many ways. Another fairly common variation is to have two peaks instead of one. Recall that the mode of a distribution is the most frequent score. A distribution having two different modes is called *bimodal*.

We would expect some distributions to be nonnormal. Recall the previous discussion of graduate student GPA in the section on range. We expect motivated students who were accepted into many graduate programs to be among the best in their field thus, a plot of the GPAs should indicate very few low GPAs. In mental health, many conditions are rare in the general population. For example, only a small percentage of people have a diagnosis of Schizophrenia or Gender Dysphoria.

Advanced note

Statisticians use various techniques to analyze data from nonnormal distributions. These strategies are beyond the scope of this basic text. In some cases, researchers will attempt to normalize the distribution if they have good evidence the measured characteristic is normally distributed in the population. In other cases, they will use strategies that do not depend on the normal curve.

Review

Define positive and negative skew.

What happens to the location of the mean, median and mode when a distribution has positive skew?

What happens to the location of the mean, median and mode when a distribution has negative skew?

Provide a brief definition of kurtosis.

Unit 3: Describing Relationships

12. Hypothesis Testing

How do we use statistics to draw conclusions?

Objectives:

Define and give an example of null and research hypotheses.

Define *significance*.

Describe two types of statistical conclusion errors.

Researchers attempt to discover relationships between variables in the real world based on samples. When researchers formulate a hypothesis, they think in terms of the real-world population but they only have a sample available. The language of hypothesis testing can seem confusing at first. If you haven't studied hypothesis testing in a while, plan to reread this section a few times.

Null Hypotheses and Research Hypotheses

A null hypothesis states that in the population there is no significant relationship between a value we calculate for one set of data and the same value in another set of data. The null hypothesis assumes any difference is due to error. In contrast, a research hypothesis proposes a significant difference. *Significant* means the difference is large enough that it is not likely due to chance and is therefore a reliable difference.

We are now set up to make a decision based on the data we obtain. If we find that our difference is not due to chance, then we find support for our research hypothesis and reject the null, or no difference, hypothesis. But if our statistic is not significant, we fail to reject the null hypothesis and do not find support for our research hypothesis. Keep in mind that hypotheses are stated in terms of the population, but we only work with samples from the population. We are using sample data to infer what is true of the population thus the statistics are called *inferential statistics*.

The Logic of Research Errors

When we obtain samples and begin to analyze data from different groups there are various sources of error. Our statistical tests are not perfect, and people vary from day to day in the data they produce. For example, people may score better on a test when they feel well compared to a day when they feel ill. In addition, we never have a sample that has the exact same properties as the entire population. The presence of errors can affect the conclusions researchers reach about their hypotheses. Two common errors are referred to as Type I and Type II.

A Type I error occurs when researchers find their data support their research hypothesis and conclude the null hypothesis is false when in fact the null hypothesis is true. They celebrate when they should not.

A Type II error occurs when researchers conclude their data do not support their research hypothesis. They fail to reject the null hypothesis when in fact the null hypothesis is false. Unfortunately, they miss out on a celebration.

Let's consider an example of program evaluation. Suppose counselors deliver a program designed to help people learn to forgive themselves. One group receives the forgiveness program and the other group receives no forgiveness intervention. After the program, clients complete a measure of self-forgiveness. The researchers hypothesized that the forgiveness program would make a significant difference. The null hypothesis simply states that there would be no difference between the groups at the conclusion of the forgiveness program.

If the researchers find a significant difference such that people in the forgiveness group had improved self-forgiveness scores compared to those who did not get treatment, then the researchers would conclude the self-forgiveness intervention was a success.

A lot of things can go wrong in such a study. For example, people in either group could read self-help books on forgiveness, or something bad could happen to a few people in one group during treatment that makes it more difficult to forgive. Also, a test used to measure self-forgiveness might not be sensitive to the changes people actually make. If anything happens to change the final self-forgiveness test score other than the self-forgiveness program, then the researchers can reach an incorrect conclusion. If people change because of a program but a test does not detect the changes, then researchers can reach an incorrect conclusion.

On the one hand, if those in the self-forgiveness group showed a high degree of improvement that was due to factors other than the forgiveness program, then a Type I error occurred. On the other hand, if the self-forgiveness test scores were not significantly different but people in the self-forgiveness group really had improved as a result of the program, then a Type II error occurred.

There are many reasons why Type I and Type II errors can occur. These are discussed in more detail in textbooks on research methods. Our purpose here is to simply understand the concepts of Type I and Type II errors.

Hypothesis Testing and Effect Size

For decades, counseling research has included the results of hypothesis testing so understanding the logic will be important to understand previous publications as well as those current publications that continue to use this approach. However, more researchers are using alternative methods to null hypothesis significance testing (NHST). An advanced discussion of the problem with NHST can be found in Cohen (1994).

One common alternative to NHST is the analysis of effect sizes. Effect sizes indicate the strength of the relationship between independent and dependent variables. The greater a change in the dependent variable linked to a change in the independent variable, the larger the effect size. By comparing effect sizes of treatments in different studies, it is possible to gain a sense about how well a particular treatment works. For example, Thomas W. Baskin and Robert D. Enright (2000) examined effect sizes for forgiveness interventions. They found an effect size of .82 for process-based group interventions.

Technical Note

You may have seen stories about science proving something to be true or false. Technically scientists do not *prove* hypotheses. Instead, scientists use the language of probability. They may report that the chances are less than 1% that a finding is false but that's still less than 100%. Scientists report results indicating *support* for their research hypotheses rather than reporting that the research hypothesis is true. The reason for such uncertainty is an appreciation of error. Researchers rely on samples. And statistics based on samples vary from sample to sample.

The word *significant* is also of concern because scientists refer to significant findings. The use of the word significant is traditional. As we can see in this chapter, significant refers to the likelihood that a finding is due to chance. It is probably more accurate to refer to a finding as *reliable* when we mean that 95% of the time a difference as large or larger than the one obtained is likely to be found 95 out of 100 times a similar study is repeated. Counselors should keep in mind that a statistically significant finding is not necessarily clinically significant. In a large sample, a difference of a few points on an intelligence test can be statistically significant but it won't necessarily make a significant difference in how well people solve problems.

Review

Researchers begin with a hypothesis called the research hypothesis, which predicts an expected outcome for a study. They often expect to find a significant relationship or difference.

Researchers create a null hypothesis, which assumes they will not find any significant difference between the variables they are studying. They hope their data allow them to reject the null hypothesis.

Researchers try to guard against making one of two types of errors. A type one error occurs when researchers conclude a finding is significant when in reality, the finding is not significant thus, they mistakenly reject a null hypothesis and conclude the research hypothesis should be supported.

A type two error occurs when researchers conclude a finding is not significant when it really is significant. They fail to reject the null hypothesis and assume they have no support for the research hypothesis.

Recently, researchers have begun to emphasize the importance of reporting and comparing effect sizes as more important than null hypothesis significance testing.

13. Correlation

What is the relationship?

Objectives:

Define *correlation*.

State the difference between a positive and negative correlation.

State the range of values for a correlation coefficient.

Explain why correlation does not imply causation.

The term *correlation* can refer to a statistic and a type of research. Understanding correlations is an important building block to many complex ideas in statistics and research methods. Our focus in this chapter is on the common correlation statistic, also called the *Pearson r*.

Counselors and researchers collect a variety of data on clients. In addition to providing basic information such as age and education, clients may complete tests and questionnaires. If we use a spreadsheet to create a database where each row represents a client and each column represents a different type of data, we will be in a position to detect relationships between two sets of data.

Consider an example. Five clients complete questionnaires about anxious and depressive symptoms. Each client has two scores—one for depression and another for anxiety. We enter the information into a spreadsheet as rows and columns. To protect client anonymity, we use a number instead of a name in the first column. For each person, we have a column for depression and a column for anxiety. We will abbreviate *depression* as *Dep* and *anxiety* as *Anx*. Our data might look like the following.

Client	Dep	Anx
01	2	4
02	5	6
03	6	7
04	7	8
05	8	6

We can see from this short list that people with higher depression scores also tend to have higher anxiety scores but the relationship is not perfect. For example, person 05 has a depression score two points higher than their anxiety score, but most people score higher on anxiety than on depression.

When two sets of scores appear to increase together, we speak of a *positive correlation,* or a *positive relationship.* When a characteristic such as age or depression can have different numerical values, the characteristic is called a *variable.* In this example, there are two variables— depression and anxiety. On average, for our sample, the two variables vary in a similar way. Higher depression is associated with higher anxiety.

Researchers examine the two sets of values and calculate a summary statistic called a *correlation coefficient.* The longer name for a common correlation statistic is the *Pearson Product Moment Correlation Coefficient* but sometimes it is referred to as the *Pearson r.* The symbol for correlation is a lower case and italicized *r*. In this example, *r* = .76. In counseling research, we normally round values to two decimal points.

Sometimes, the relationship between two variables is negative. For example, the relationship between depression and self-esteem is often negative. As depression increases, self-esteem decreases. An example of a negative correlation would be written as *r* = -.45. The minus sign tells us that as one variable increases, the other variable decreases. The relationship is commonly described in articles as an *inverse relationship*.

An example from published research is the relationship between perceived stress and humility couples experience as they transition to parenthood. As a part of their work, Jennifer Ripley and her research team (2016) found that the correlation between a measure of perceived stress and a measure of humility ranged from -.33 to -.45, which indicates that high stress is associated with low humility.

Relationship Strength

The relationship between two variables not only varies in a positive or negative direction but it also varies in terms of strength. Large *r* values indicate a stronger relationship. When *r* = .75 or -.75, the relationship is of equal strength but in different directions. Relationships with a low number such as *r* = .15 or *r* = -.11 indicate weak relationships.

When *r* values are at or near zero, we say there is no relationship between the values. For example, we may find no relationship between scores on questionnaires about humility and depression.

Relationships and Significance

Researchers report a probability value along with the *r* value. The statistical concept of probability is complex. In practice, statistical software calculates probability values associated with various statistics. The probability values are identified by the lower case and italicized letter *p*.

A probability value provides readers with a sense of a statistic's reliability or stability if researchers were to calculate the statistic for another sample of a similar size. It is traditional to refer to a statistical finding as significant or not significant. Recall that the term *significant* can be misleading because what counts as statistically significant may not be clinically significant in counseling.

A statistic like the Pearson *r* can range from -1.0 to +1.0. The larger the value of the statistic, the stronger the relationship. The correlation value of -.65 is as strong as .65. The size of the relationship and the size of the sample are factors in determining the probability that a researcher would find a correlation of the same size or larger in a future sample. Traditionally, researchers consider a correlation to be significant if the value is likely to be the same size or larger 95% of the time a study is conducted. Put another way, if researchers have only a 5% chance that an obtained correlation is as large as the one they found by chance, then the researchers usually conclude the correlation is significant.

Software programs usually provide probability values up to three decimal places but researchers ought to decide on the value they will count as significant before conducting a study. If we set our value in advance then we examine the *p* value to see if it is above or below the 5% chance level. The

5% level is written as .05. If the probability of obtaining r = .65 is .02, then we find that r = .65 is significant. In writing a report, we may use the following phrase.

The relationship between depression and anxiety is significant (r = .76, p <.05).

If a relationship was not statistically significant, then the researcher would change the interpretive sentence. Here is an example of a nonsignificant statement:

The relationship between depression and intelligence was not significant (r = .09, p > .05).

Notice the less-than and greater-than symbols used to compare the value to the significance value of p =.05. When p is less than .05 we mean the chances of finding a difference this large or larger in another study with participants drawn from the same population by chance alone are less than 5%.

Reading Research

I have used the .05 level (5% level) of significance in these examples. Other common levels of significance in counseling research include .01 (1% level) and .001 (.1% level). In very large samples, researchers sometimes use stricter significance levels because small differences can be detected as significant more easily at the .05 level. The reason these significance levels are used is a matter of tradition. There is no particular reason why a person could not choose .02, but researchers stay with tradition.

Correlation Sizes

Researchers sometimes use rough guidelines to describe the size of a correlation value. Keep in mind that these are very rough descriptors. As with many things in life, context is important. My purpose in providing these guidelines is to suggest what a researcher may consider when the words are used in research reports.

Small = .25 or less

Moderate = between .25 and .40

Large = .40 or greater

Most spreadsheets that come with office programs will calculate the Pearson r values and probability values.

Correlation methods

I have written about the Pearson r, which is the most common correlation coefficient. Researchers reporting the Pearson r should check that the data are at least at an interval scale of measurement and normally distributed. You may read about other correlation coefficients used when data are not normally distributed. For example, the point biserial correlation can be used when one variable is dichotomous (e.g., mothers, fathers) and another variable is continuous (e.g., scores on a test). Dichotomous variables can be naturally occurring variables or those created by a researcher such as organizing reported ages into two age groups. The Spearman Rank Order Correlation Coefficient and Kendall's tau can be calculated for ranked sets of data. Recall that rankings, like numerical scores provided by judges, are on an ordinal scale. Cramer's V and Phi are examples of correlation coefficients for nominal data.

Correlation and Explanation

Researchers usually report the correlation statistic as an r value. But there are times when we may want to communicate a specific finding about the relationship between two variables. Suppose a study finds the relationship between the IQ scores of mothers and their oldest child is .5. When the .5 value is squared, it equals .25, which can be converted to a percent: 25%. Researchers might say that 25% of a child's IQ is explained by their mother's IQ, or, written another way, the IQs of mothers and their oldest child share 25% of the variance.

Correlation and Causation

A common error in thinking about correlations is to conclude that a change in one variable causes a change in another variable. The fact that two variables have a strong relationship does not mean the relationship is a cause-effect type of relationship. For example, traumatic life experiences may cause a person to experience both depression and anxiety. The fact that depression and anxiety are correlated does not necessarily mean depression causes anxiety. Neither does it necessarily mean that anxiety causes depression.

Advanced Reading Note

In this chapter I have discussed the correlation between two variables commonly identified in text books as X and Y. It is possible to expand our understanding of a variable by looking at multiple correlations. For example, suppose we wanted to look at many factors that are associated with PTSD. We could examine possible factors linked to PTSD symptoms such as age of first traumatic experience, severity of traumatic experience, duration of the traumatic experience, and so forth. Each of these variables can be considered as a part of an X variable set. Within the set, the individual variables are identified with a subscript such as X_1, X_2, and so on. The term for this statistical analysis is *Multiple Correlation*. There are different statistical methods to calculate multiple correlations. In reading about multiple correlation, look for the variables in the set of X variables, which are sometimes called *independent, explanatory*, or *predictor* variables. And look for the Y variable sometimes called a *dependent, predicted*, or *outcome* variable. The researchers report which variables best explain or predict the variable that is to be explained or predicted.

When reading newer articles, you will often find p values reported as an exact number such as $p = .025$, which is compared to a conventional significance level such as .01 or .05. By tradition, researchers round most statistics to two decimal places but p values are reported up to three decimal places. When software reports $p = .000$ it is reported as $p < .001$ because p does not equal zero.

Review

We can study the direction and strength of the relationship between two variables by calculating a Pearson r correlation coefficient.

The Pearson r values range from -1.0 to +1.0.

Positive r values indicate that as one variable increases or decreases, so does the other.

Negative r values indicate that as one value increases, the other value decreases.

The size of the Pearson r value indicates the strength of the relationship.

Researchers consider the probability that the obtained r value is due to chance.

If the p value is less than a cutoff value, such as .05, then the researcher considers the relationship to be significant. But if the p value is larger than the cut off value, then the relationship is not considered significant.

Some values that are statistically significant are not clinically significant. In very large samples, a small correlation value can be statistically significant but of little practical significance.

The fact that two variables are significantly correlated does not mean that a change in one variable causes a change in another variable. Correlation does not imply causation.

14. Charts

How can we picture relationships?

Objectives:

Identify the x and y axes on a graph.

Describe the pattern for positive and negative linear relationships.

Whether you are examining data in a private practice or conducting research on large groups, it is often helpful to look at the data. Examining a graph of the data reveals the nature or pattern of a relationship. Suppose we plot clients' scores from questionnaires about depression and anxiety to create a simple graph. A standard practice in statistics is to label the horizontal axis of a graph as the x-axis and the vertical axis as the y-axis. In our example, it does not matter which variable we identify as X or Y.

To create a graph, we simply draw a grid or use a software program to plot the scores. In our example, scores on the x-axis will be depression and they may range from 0 to 9. Scores on the y-axis will be anxiety and those scores may also range from 0 to 9. Each point on the graph represents one person. Each person has two scores—one for depression on the x-axis and one for anxiety on the y-axis. For example, the person at the left side of the grid has a depression score of 1 and an anxiety score of 2.

Our example of a positive relationship looks like the following. If you try to draw a straight diagonal line close to the points on the graph you will not be able to connect each point. Our inability to draw a perfectly straight line that would connect all dots means we have less than a perfect correlation between the measure of depression and the measure of anxiety. The line represents a trend moving from the lower left to the upper right. The correlation is .85.

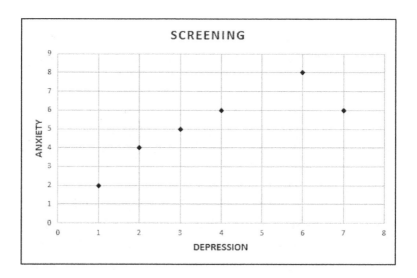

Following is a chart showing a negative relationship between depression and self-esteem. The correlation is -.95. In general, the lower the depression score, the higher the self-esteem score. Again, you cannot draw a perfectly straight line connecting each point, but you get a sense of the linear trend for the sample.

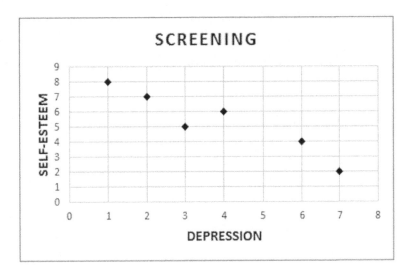

Some plots of data are so scattered that it is not possible to draw a line through the data points. The relationship of X and Y variables would be at or near zero in these cases. Researchers do not usually include plots of nonsignificant results in reports or articles.

In advanced texts, you can read about nonlinear relationships. One variable can be related to another variable in various curvilinear relationships. For example, curves may be U-shaped or S-shaped.

Review

The relationship between two variables X and Y can be depicted on a graph.

Often, it is possible to draw a straight-line close to all the data points to reveal a linear trend.

Linear trends are common in counseling research.

15. Predictions

How can we make predictions?

Objectives:

Identify a common method of predicting scores on one variable from scores on another variable.

Identify the term associated with errors in prediction.

If we know the relationship between two variables in previous studies, we can use that information to make predictions about future studies. For example, suppose counselors have school test records documenting a strong positive relationship between scores on a vocabulary test and scores on a reading test. The counselors can use a formula to predict unknown reading scores when they know vocabulary scores and the history of their correlation with reading scores in previous samples.

We should use caution when estimating or predicting possible scores when we do not have actual scores. Predicted scores on tests are subject to errors of estimation, which should be calculated and reported. In general, first year college GPA can be predicted from high school GPA but the prediction is not perfect.

The higher the correlation between two variables, the more accurate the prediction will be if the new sample is similar to the sample in the original study. If you have five years' worth of data about students' high school and college GPAs and attempt to predict the college GPAs of this year's high school graduates you will probably have a good estimate if the current graduates are similar to the graduates from previous years. Of course, you will need to use the same tests and they should attend the same colleges.

The error associated with prediction is known as the *Standard Error of Estimate* (*SEE*). Researchers usually report a predicted score along with a range of one or two standard errors. The standard errors around a predicted score conform to the properties of a normal curve. This error range is known as a *confidence interval* (CI).

Using our knowledge of the normal curve, we will find that approximately 68% of the time we perform a similar study, a predicted score will fall within plus or minus 1 *SEE* and 95% of the time, the predicted score will fall within plus or minus 2 *SEEs*.

Here's an example of an *SEE* calculation and a way to phrase a statement about a predicted score. The phrase is a cautious prediction of a score within 2 SEEs of a predicted score of 3.3. The *SEE* was found to be .05, so two times .05 = .1. To find the score above and below 3.3, we subtract 2 *SEEs* from 3.3 to get 3.2 (3.3 -.1 = 3.2) and we add 2 SEEs to 3.3 to get 3.4 (3.3 + .1 = 3.4). The 95% confidence interval is 3.2 to 3.4.

Based on fictional historical data, students who graduate high school with a 3.5 GPA typically end their first year of college with a GPA in the range of 3.2 to 3.4 (*SEE* = .05).

Advanced Reading Note

Recall that in the chapter on correlation, I referred to Multiple Correlation. In practice, researchers usually include multiple variables when attempting to predict or estimate performance on another variable. For example, in counseling outcome research, we may attempt to predict successful outcomes from a set of predictor variables such as number of treatment sessions, commitment to counseling, hope, and other variables.

Review

If counselors know the correlation between two sets of data such as test scores, they can predict scores on a future test if the new sample is similar to the sample used to calculate the correlation.

Because scores on tests vary from sample to sample, researchers must calculate and report the Standard Error of Estimate (SEE).

The SEE provides a range or confidence interval within which a predicted score is expected to fall.

In research, scientists usually predict scores and outcomes based on the relationship between a set of predictors and the value they wish to predict.

Unit 4: Discovering Group Differences

16. *t* Tests

How can we analyze differences between two groups?

Objectives:

Identify three types of *t* tests.

Define *degrees of freedom*.

The two-group study is a building block for more complex research designs. In its simplest form, a researcher randomly assigns people to two different groups, presents a counseling intervention to one group but not the other group (control group), and measures each person (both groups) on some measure expected to change in response to the counseling intervention. If the groups are significantly different on the measurement, then you can conclude, all things being equal, the counseling intervention probably caused the significant difference in the measurement.

Counselors may wish to know the value of bibliotherapy (reading materials such as self-help books outside of counseling) for helping people develop more self-confidence. In a two-group study, participants could be randomly assigned to one of two conditions. One group, the control group, meets a counselor, consents to the study, receives a self-help book to read, and then returns to complete a questionnaire about self-confidence. The other group meets the counselor, consents to the study, but does not get a self-help book. Instead, they read other neutral materials. The people in the no-bibliotherapy group return at the same time as those in the self-help group, and everyone completes the same self-confidence questionnaire. If the group that received bibliotherapy significantly improved their scores on a reliable measure of self-confidence, we may consider adding a self-confidence bibliotherapy intervention to our counseling practice. Now let's consider the relevant hypotheses and a common statistical test.

Research question

> What is the effect of bibliotherapy on self-confidence?

Research hypothesis

> If participants participate in bibliotherapy (read a self-help book) to build self-confidence then their self-confidence scores will increase compared to those who do not participate in bibliotherapy

Null hypothesis

> There will be no significant difference in self-confidence for those in the bibliotherapy or no bibliotherapy conditions on the population means of self-confidence ($p < .05$).

The self-confidence study is based on two different groups of people. The analysis of differences is commonly done based on the differences between the average score of each group. You can simply subtract the mean of one group from the other and see if there is a difference. Small differences are likely due to chance alone.

A statistical test known as the *t test* considers the size of the sample and the standard deviation for each group. Statistics programs compare the obtained differences to differences required for significance. Again, by *significance,* researchers mean differences that are large enough that they are not likely due to chance. Our typical criterion is a difference that will be found 95% of the time we repeat the study. That is, we want a difference large enough that there is less than a 5% chance (.05) the difference occurs by chance.

The *t* Tests

The *t*-test allows researchers to compare the sample means for two groups. If the means are significantly different then researchers may conclude that the population means are also different and reject their null hypothesis in favor of the research hypothesis provided their design was appropriate. Researchers use different *t* tests depending on the research designs. I will present three *t* tests: independent, dependent, single sample

Independent-samples *t* Tests

If we want to study differences between two groups that are formed by randomly assigning people to the groups we can use an independent samples *t* test. The tests may be one-tailed or two-tailed. In a one-tailed test the researchers have a reason to believe that one mean will likely be higher than the other mean. In a two-tailed test, the researchers examine whether the differences are significant regardless of which difference is higher. In a study I conducted with Tom Huberty (Sutton & Huberty, 1984), we wished to examine mean differences between two groups of teachers (regular and special education) on measures of teacher stress and job satisfaction. The measures are sometimes called *dependent measures*. Dependent measures are tests or other measures that purport to measure the dependent variable. In an experiment, the groups represent two conditions of an independent variable but in a comparison study, the groups are two conditions of a status variable sometimes called a *classification variable*. In our study, type of teacher was a classification variable. We did not control which teachers were in regular or special education.

Dependent-samples *t* Test.

When two groups are matched in some way a different *t* test is used. In some cases, the two groups may be matched on an important variable that is correlated with the dependent variable in an experiment. In other cases, the same participants obtain scores on two measures at different times such as before and after treatment. The dependent-samples *t* test is sometimes referred to by the following names: matched-pairs, paired-samples, correlated groups, repeated-measures.

Here is an example. Researchers (Sutton, Koller & Christian, 1982) wished to compare two commonly used measures of intelligence. Each participant took both intelligence tests. Their mean scores were compared, and no significant differences were found. The two tests appeared to measure intelligence to the same degree even though the tests used different tasks.

One-sample *t* Test.

The one-sample *t* test is different because researchers work with only one sample. This test can be used when researchers want to examine whether the mean of a sample is significantly different from some specific value. If a published test is used we can obtain the means and standard deviations for test results from previously published studies. Suppose you look at student achievement on a national achievement test that has known means and standard deviations for representative samples of students at all age levels. The information about the national sample can be used as a standard against which our new sample can be compared using a one-sample t test.

Degrees of Freedom

When comparing samples drawn from a population, it is important to realize that sample size can affect the outcome of a study. When we make inferences about a population value from a sample, we wish to be conservative. Students of statistics often find the *degrees of freedom* (*df*) concept difficult to understand, and many teachers confess it is difficult to explain. Here's one attempt. You will find different explanations in other textbooks.

Suppose counselors in an agency have the opportunity to schedule a group on one of five days, Monday through Friday. After Monday is chosen, there are four days left. After Monday and Tuesday are chosen, there are three days left. By the time four days—Monday through Thursday—are chosen, there is no choice left. After Thursday, there is no variance in days. The degrees of freedom for the choice of days for the group is $5 - 4 = 1$.

For two independent samples, the *df* is the number of participants minus two when the variances between two groups is equal ($df = N - 2$). For paired-samples and one-sample tests, the *df* is the number of participants minus one ($df = N - 1$). When reporting t-test results, the number in parenthesis following the letter t is the value of *df* used. If *df* = 18, then it is written as $t(18)$.

Effect Size

Effect sizes are very important because they indicate the strength of the relationship between the independent variable and the dependent variable. A common measure of effect size used with two-group studies is *Cohen's d*. In a two-group study having a counseling intervention group and a comparison group, the means of the two groups are subtracted then divided by a value that represents the pooled variance of each group. The resulting *d* statistic provides a measure of the size of the treatment effect.

Researchers refer to ranges of effect size as follows (e.g., Warner, 2013):

> Small: Less than or equal to .20
>
> Medium: Near .50; between .20 and .79
>
> Large: Above .80

Written Example

Here is an example of how *t* test results may be written. All numbers are fictitious.

We found that bibliotherapy for mild depression ($M = 15$, $SD = 2$) was significantly better than no treatment ($M = 11$, $SD = 2$), $t(18) = 4.08$, $p < .05$, $d = 1.50$, two-tailed.

Let's unpack the sentence reporting the results. There are two groups of a treatment variable. The mean for the bibliotherapy group (15) was 4 points higher than the mean for of those in the no treatment group (11). The standard deviations are the same. There were 20 people in the study. We know this because the $df = 18$ and df for two groups is found by subtracting 2 from the number of people in the study ($20 - 2 = 18$). The *t* value of 4.08 is significant (less than .05) and the effect size is large ($d = 1.50$ is above .80). The researchers did not predict one group to be higher than another based on the use of a two-tailed test.

Additional note

The *t* in *t* test is italicized and lower case. An upper case *T* is reserved for a type of test score.

Review for *t* tests

Assumptions for *t* tests:

- The values are measured on an interval or ratio scale.
- The sample values represent a random sample from the population values.
- The population of values is normally distributed.
- The variances of the groups are about the same (homogeneous).

Three different *t*-test procedures are available: one-sample, independent samples, and dependent samples.

The *t* test is reported with the following values: *t* statistic, degrees of freedom, *p* value, effect size.

17. Analysis of Variance

How can we analyze differences among multiple groups?

Objectives:

> Describe a procedure for analyzing differences among three or more groups.
>
> Describe the basic purpose of post hoc tests.

A lot of work is involved in preparing and carrying out a research study. In addition to the work of the research team, we must consider the commitment of the participants. For these reasons, it is rare to conduct simple studies involving a few people divided into two groups. The purpose of this chapter is to introduce a family of statistical procedures based on the analysis of variances.

At a basic level, the word *variance* means difference. The difference of interest to us in this chapter is the difference that represents improvement or change related to some aspect of counseling. Differences are usually examined in terms of group averages, which are the mean scores on some type of measurement. Consider a three-group example.

A research team wishes to determine the best treatment for Posttraumatic Stress Disorder (PTSD). Two new programs have been developed and are considered better than the old one in use. The only difference between the two new programs is that one uses medication and the other does not. To test for differences, we design a study with three groups, which we identify as N (new program), M (new program plus medication) and O (old program). Participants are told about the programs, and after giving consent, they are randomly assigned to one of the three treatment groups.

Here's how we might phrase the research question and hypotheses.

Research question

What is the effect of type of counseling program on PTSD symptoms?

Research hypothesis

If participants receive a New PTSD program then their PTSD symptoms will be lower than those who participate in the traditional Old Program.

Null hypothesis

There will be no significant difference for type of PTSD program on the population means of PTSD symptoms as measured by a PTSD scale ($p < .05$).

Data Analysis

At the end of the study, data are collected. The research team then begins to analyze the data. After entering the data into a database, the team needs to select an appropriate statistical test. They could analyze differences between each pair of groups using a series of three *t* tests. The reason researchers do not use this approach is because conducting a lot of tests on one set of data increases the statistical odds of finding a difference. This phenomenon is called *fishing,* and the problem is called the *family-wise error rate.* The more statistical tests you conduct, the more likely it is that you will find a significant result.

The solution to the problem of multiple tests is to conduct one overall test first. A test developed by Fisher is named in his honor as the *F*-test and the procedure is called the *analysis of variance* referred to as *ANOVA*. The calculation results in an *F* statistic, which can be compared to known distributions of the statistic to discover how large an *F* value needs to be to determine that there is a significant difference between the group means in a study.

The *F*-statistic is the result of a ratio comparing the differences between the groups to overall differences of all the people in the study. In our example, if the new programs N or M are better than the old program (O), then scores on tests of PTSD ought to be significantly better for groups N and M than scores on the same tests for group O.

The differences between the groups is a matter of calculating the variance among the means. In our study, there are three groups, each having a mean. We could also find the average of the means (the mean of the means) by adding the means together and dividing by three. Recall that variance tells us the average differences of scores from a mean. At this point, we are interested in the difference of the group means from the average or overall mean. The overall mean is sometimes called the *Grand Mean*. The variance of the group means from the Grand Mean is called the Between Groups Variance. Recall that another name for variance is mean squares. Sometimes Between Groups variance is called *Between Groups Mean Squares* written as MS_{bet}. The MS_{bet} represents the effects of treatment plus some amount of error.

The differences between the group means will tell us which group improved more than the others, but people vary in many characteristics. In this study, we can expect PTSD symptoms to vary for all the people in the study. To determine the effect of the programs on PTSD symptoms we need to consider the normal variation of the people in the study regardless of their group assignment. This analysis is called *within groups variance*. Within Groups variance is also called *Within Groups Mean Squares* written as MS_{with}. The MS_{with} represents error.

The F value is obtained by dividing the average differences between the group means by the average differences of individual scores from the overall score mean. F = Between Groups Variance divided by Within Groups Variance. This can also be stated as F = Between Groups Mean Squares divided by Within Groups Mean Squares. If we use abbreviations like you would see in textbooks and reports, the equation would appear as $F = MS_{bet} / MS_{with}$.

Recall that in the t test procedure, the t statistic varies by group size, and we needed to consider the degrees of freedom, where the df for each group was $N - 1$. In the ANOVA procedure, there are two df values to consider—one for each component in the F ratio. The df for the variance between groups is the number of groups minus one. The df for the within groups variance is the number of participants in the study minus the number of groups.

Software programs provide the results, which include the values for the two variance components of the F ratio along with the df values, the F statistic, and the p value for the F statistic. The statistics programs will also provide an estimate of effect size.

Because we are examining the results from a study of only one variable, this type of ANOVA is called a one-way ANOVA. Another word for a variable is *factor,* so you may see this ANOVA referred to as a *single-factor ANOVA*. If we had two treatment variables, we would use a two-way ANOVA.

Effect size

Recall that effect sizes indicate the strength of the relationship between the independent variable and a dependent variable. In this study, the independent variable is counseling intervention, which is varied three ways (the three groups N, M, O). The dependent variable of PTSD is represented by scores on a PTSD test. There are different measures of effect size. A common *ES* reported with ANOVA is partial eta squared, which is written using the Greek letter η^2.

Post hoc tests

Finally, if our *F* statistic is significant—that is, $p < .05$—then we conclude that at least one comparison between the groups is significant (not likely due to chance). Recall that there are three possible comparisons in a three-group study:

N and M

N and O

M and O

Because we first tested for overall significance, we are entitled to conduct tests on the differences between each group. We can use the familiar *t* test or one of a number of other tests available in different software programs. Some common names for post hoc tests you might see in published reports include Tukey, Bonferroni, and Scheffé. These tests are known as *post hoc tests* meaning that they are only conducted after the main analysis has been completed.

Reporting Results

Here's an example of how to phrase a significant finding related to our fictitious study.

We conducted a one-way ANOVA to examine possible differences in PTSD symptoms following treatment. The results indicated the presence of a significant difference among the groups, $F(2,27) = 5.06$, $p < .05$, $\eta^2 = .22$. A follow-up comparison using the Tukey HSD test revealed significant differences. PTSD symptoms for those in the Old program group were significantly lower ($M = 50$, $SD = 10$) than for those in either the New program group ($M = 67$, $SD = 11$) or the New Program plus medication group ($M = 60$, $SD = 12$).

Notes on Reading Advanced Analyses

Researchers have a variety of procedures available to analyze variances among research groups. In this chapter, I presented the example of a one-way ANOVA, which examined differences among the groups of one independent variable on the dependent variable mean scores. It is possible to add independent variables each having two or more groups. The ANOVA for a study with two independent variables is called a two-way ANOVA. The results are often reported using numbers that tell how many groups are in each variable. For example, a study of three kinds of a therapy variable and two types of a presentation variable (e.g., individual vs. group) would be written as 3 X 2. This logic can be expanded to three and four-way ANOVAs for studies having three and four independent variables respectively.

An even more complex approach is to add more than one dependent variable to the above examples. For example, suppose we examined two different treatments for depression by measuring improvement on two dependent measures of depression such as a measure of thoughts and a measure of physical symptoms. The name for ANOVAs with two or more dependent variables is *MANOVA* (*Multivariate Analysis of Variance*). As in the case of ANOVA, MANOVAs can be analyzed for one, two, or more independent variables thus you may read about one-way MANOVAs, two-way MANOVAs, and so forth.

Finally, researchers can assess the influence of other variables called *covariates* on the dependent variable. For example, age may be associated with therapy outcome. This possible association can be tested by treating age as a covariate. The procedure is called ANCOVA where the *C* represents the fact that the data analyst included one or more covariates in the data analysis. Similarly, covariates can be added to MANCOVAs when another variable thought to influence the dependent measures has been included in the database.

Review of ANOVA

ANOVA procedures assume the following:

- The participants in each of the groups in a study are drawn from a normally distributed population.
- There is one independent variable having two or more independent groups. The participants in the groups are in only one group.
- The group sizes are equal (or at least close to equal).
- There is one dependent variable and the values are normally distributed.
- The values on the dependent variable are measured on an interval or ratio scale.

- The samples are drawn from populations that have a common variance.

Results of ANOVA are reported with an F value, degrees of freedom (df) for groups and the total sample, a p value, and a measure of effect size.

If the overall ANOVA results in a significant difference, then a post hoc test is used to examine differences between each pair of group means.

18. Chi-Square

How can we analyze frequency data?

Objectives:

State when a chi-square test may be used.

Identify a common measure of effect size reported with chi-square analyses.

Identify the components of a phrase reporting chi-square results.

The chi-square test is one of several tests researchers can use to look for significant differences when data are not measured on an interval or ratio scale of measurement. The chi-square test is used for frequency data. The Greek letter *chi* (χ) is pronounced like KIGH and rhymes with *pie*.

We can use a chi-square test when we have two categorical variables. For example, we could examine the frequency of people with depression in a community by studying people who were treated compared to those who were not treated. And we could compare those who exercise at high or low frequency levels during a week. Our null hypothesis is that the variables are independent of each other. Our research hypothesis is simply the logical opposite stating that we expect to find a relationship.

Statistics programs will report a chi-square value along with the degrees of freedom (*df*), a *p* value, and a measure of effect size. This simple design is a 2 X 2 design. There are rows of data for the treated and untreated groups and columns for low and high frequency of exercise. The table organizing the data is called a *contingency table.*

	Low Exercise	High Exercise
Treated	20	30
Untreated	20	30

The *df* is the number of rows (r) minus one times the number of columns (c) minus one. In this simple example, we have two categories of treatment and two groups of exercise. The *df* equals $(r-1) \times (c-1)$ so $1 \times 1 = 1$ thus, *df* = 1. Assume that we consider a *p* value less than .05 to be significant. Large chi-square values represent large differences between the groups. If the chi-square value results in a *p* value less than .05, we reject the null hypothesis and find support for the research hypothesis.

A common measure of effect size reported with chi-square is Cramer's V. As with other effect sizes, Cramer's V is a measure of association between variables. A rough guide to descriptions of effect size for Cramer's V is as follows:

Small = 0.1

Medium = 0.3

Large = 0.5

Notes

The chi-square test I described is also called the *Pearson Chi-Square Test* and the *chi-square test for independence.*

The chi-square test requires a minimum of 5 cases per cell.

A different but related chi-square test is the *Goodness of fit test*. This test can be used with one sample to determine if the sample data called the *observed* data are consistent with hypothesized or *expected* data.

Review

Researchers can use a chi-square test to examine associations between categorical variables yielding frequency data.

A common effect size statistic reported with chi-square results is Cramer's V.

The results of a chi-square analysis include the chi-square statistic, degrees of freedom, a *p* value, and a measure of effect size.

Unit 5: Understanding Test Scores

19. Test Scores

What are some common test scores?

Objectives:

Describe common test scores including the mean and standard deviation.

Define *Standard Error of Measurement.*

Testing has been a part of human experience since ancient times. Every year children take tests at school. Adults take tests to obtain licenses and demonstrate skills. Counselors use tests to assess achievement, intelligence, personality traits, and personal strengths. Counselors are often called upon to explain test scores to clients, parents, and interested groups.

The purpose of this chapter is to review the characteristics of common test scores. There are various ways to consider what a test score means. In this chapter, I will focus on scores from tests that allow a comparison to a reference group, known as a *norming* or *standardization sample.* I will also assume the score distribution of the norming sample is the same as the normal curve.

Recall that scores having a normal distribution have the same mean, median, and mode in the center of the bell-shaped distribution. Half, or 50%, of the scores are below the mean, and 50% of the scores are above the mean. Also recall that the properties of the normal curve are such that 68% of scores fall between -1 and +1 standard deviations (SD) from the mean; 95% of scores fall between -2 and +2 standard deviations from the mean; and 99% of scores fall between -3 and +3 standard deviations from the mean.

Basic Test Terms

The word *test* in counseling is usually reserved for published assessments that have been standardized on large representative samples. These include tests of achievement, intelligence, and personality. However, the word *test* also refers to those classroom exams created by teachers and professors, so it is important to understand what people mean by a test.

Measure is a generic term often used in research articles for a set of questions that may or may not be standardized. A research measure can include a standardized test such as a published test of intelligence or achievement. *Measure* can also refer to a researcher's creation of a scale or questionnaire. For example, a researcher may create a five-item measure to assess a trait like self-esteem or courage.

The word *item* refers to a specific question or statement on a measure that produces a score. Each spelling word on a spelling test is an item. Each problem on a math test is an item. Each statement about personality on a personality test is an item. Items may have one correct answer as in true-or-false and multiple-choice items. Items can also ask test takers to choose a range of responses such as a five-point response ranging from *Strongly Agree* to *Strongly Disagree*.

Test scores are obtained by adding the scores for each item. Sometimes the scores are added to form subtest scores. For example, a popular personality test called *the Big Five* has five subscales: Openness, Conscientiousness, Extroversion, Agreeableness, Neuroticism. Counselors and researchers usually interpret scores for each subscale. There are actually many versions of the Big Five. One short version has only 10 items. Longer versions include subtests for each of the Big Five.

Raw Scores

Raw scores are the actual scores people obtain on a test. If a student defines 6 terms on a quiz that contains 10 items, she has a raw score of 6. We cannot interpret her score without knowing more information.

Percentiles and Percentile Ranks

A simple way of communicating scores is in terms of a percentile rank (PR). Percentile Ranks range from 1 to 99. The mean is 50. A PR of 50 means that 50% of people taking the test score below the mean. Common PR for scores related to the three standard deviations are as follows.

-3 *SD* < *PR* 1

-2 *SD* = *PR* 2 (almost)

-1 *SD* = *PR* 16

0 *SD* = *PR* 50

+1 *SD* = *PR* 84

+2 *SD* = *PR* 98 (approximately)

+3 *SD* = *PR* > 99

The difference between the terms *percentile* and *percentile rank* can be illustrated in two statements. A score of 100 has a percentile rank of 75 means that 75% of the population had scores less than 100. The 75th percentile is

100 means that 75% of the population had scores of 100 or less. A percentile is a point that divides a distribution. A percentile rank is a percent number indicating the percentage of cases below a given value. Percentiles are measured on the same scale of measurement as the original variable. Percentile ranks are ordinal data. Percentile ranks are useful for reporting scores to individuals.

Standard Scores

z-scores

The simple building block for standard scores is a z-score. Based on the basic properties of the normal curve, z-scores have a mean of zero and a standard deviation of 1. Given our knowledge of the normal curve, 99% of z-scores will fall between -3 and +3 standard deviations. It is not common to find tests that use z-scores because of the negative numbers. The letter z is lower case and italicized.

T-scores

T-scores are like z-scores but avoid negative numbers by setting the mean at 50 and the standard deviation at 10. The letter T is upper case and italicized. T-scores are common in measures of personality.

IQ scores

Contemporary IQ tests use deviation IQ scores. These standard scores have a mean of 100 and a standard deviation of 15.

Stanine scores

Some schools have used stanine scores. The term *stanine* means standard nines and has scores ranging from 1 to 9, with $M = 5$ and $SD = 2$.

Sten scores

Some scores are reported as stens. A sten, or standard ten score, has $M = 5.5$ and $SD = 2$.

NCE scores

NCE is an abbreviation for Normal Curve Equivalent. The scores are commonly used in school settings. The scores can be compared to the normal curve and range from 1 to 99, with $M = 50$ and $SD = 21.06$.

Developmental Scores

Age scores are sometimes reported for children. An age score compares a test score to those obtained by other children of the same age. For example, a test age score of 8-5 refers to an average score obtained by children aged 8 years and 5 months. Notice that age scores use hyphens followed by a number representing one of the 12 months of the year. Scores are rounded to the nearest month. The scores are imprecise compared to standard scores. Age scores do not make much sense when applied to adults.

Grade equivalent (GE) scores are sometimes reported for children in elementary and secondary schools. A GE score compares a test score to those obtained by other children of the same grade. For example, a GE score of 6.7 refers to an average score obtained by children in the seventh month of sixth grade. Notice that GE scores use decimals for the 10 months of a school year. Scores are rounded to the nearest month. The scores are imprecise compared to standard scores. It is not accurate to describe an adult's achievement level in terms of scores on a child's test of achievement when the adult's scores are compared to children's.

Score Error

All scores contain errors. Test publishers report the Standard Error of Measurement, or SEM. The SEM reflects the theoretical range of a person's score if he or she were to take the test on a repeated basis. Theoretically, if someone takes a test 100 times, their scores would be within 1 standard deviation of their obtained score 68% of the time. Suppose a person takes an achievement test having an SEM of 3 and obtains a score of 90. Based on the properties of the normal curve, 68% of the time they retake the test, they should obtain scores between 87 and 93 (90 -3 or +3 points). If we wanted to be more cautious and consider a range of 2 SEMs, then we would add and subtract 6 points, giving an obtained score of 90 a range of 84 to 96. We could write that on retesting, his score would probably fall between 84 and 96 about 95% of the time. The range of the SEM above and below the obtained score is called a confidence interval (CI).

In test research, scientists consider the average SEM for test results. For example, Kara Styck and Shana Walsh reviewed scoring errors made by examiners administering the Wechsler Adult Intelligence Scale IV. As a part of their analysis, they reported the average measurement error for the scale was plus or minus 3 IQ points (2016).

Technical Note

Spread sheets and statistical software programs can calculate scores from a data set. The z-score is the basis for other standard scores. Most scoring systems prefer to avoid the negative numbers in z-scores. If you can calculate a z-score you can use formulas to calculate other scores.

To calculate a z-score, subtract an obtained score (X) from the mean (M) and divide by the standard deviation (SD) of the test. The formula is as follows: $z = (X - M) / SD$. Here's an example. A person earns a score of 60 on a test with a mean of 50 and a standard deviation of 10. Thus, 60 – 50 = 10, and 10 / 10 = 1. The z-score is 1.

To convert a z-score to a T-score, multiply the z-score by 10 and add or subtract 50. A z-score of 1 equals a T-score of 60. $T = 10z + 50$, so $T = (10 \times 1) + 50 = 60$.

Review

In addition to the raw score, test publishers report one or more standard scores.

Test scores vary; thus, it is important to consider measurement error when reading about or reporting test scores.

20. Test Score Reliability

Can you trust the scores?

Objectives:

Define *reliability* related to test scores.

State the range of a reliability statistic.

Describe common methods of determining reliability.

Art disagreed with his boss about the width of a concrete girder, which John had measured twice and ended up with a different length each time. Then Art noticed the numbers on John's ruler were misprinted. They laughed as John trashed the bad ruler. My dad (Art) loved to tell this story. It's a good example of problems with reliable measurement.

Here's an important phrase: *Reliability is a property of scores not tests*.

The question "Is the test reliable?" has no answer. We can only report the reliability of scores using the test with specific samples and under specific testing conditions. Many people in counseling and related fields do not talk or write as if there is a difference between test reliability and reliability as a property of scores and not tests.

For several reasons, people get different scores when they take the same test again. Scores vary. Variation in scores represents error. Studies of test scores taken from large representative samples allow test researchers to estimate the typical amount of error associated with a test score. This value is known as *measurement error*.

If a test truly measures intelligence, then it ought to yield the same score every time. In practice, scores on tests of intelligence are fairly reliable. In this case, reliability means that the scores are stable from one test time to another.

Factors affecting score reliability

Many factors can influence the reliability of a test score. Here are a few examples:

- The wording of test items.
- Variations in the test instructions provided by the test administrator.
- Variations in the test environment such as temperature, humidity, noise, and comfortable seating.
- Variations in a person due to illness, pain, medication, or stress.

Reliability statistics

The reliability of test scores ranges from zero to one. The number is known as a *reliability coefficient* and is a correlation coefficient with only positive numbers. A perfectly reliable set of scores would have a coefficient of 1.0. In practice, tests of intelligence and achievement usually have reliability values above .90. Scores on tests of personality characteristics and mental health conditions vary more than scores on cognitive tests thus lower reliability values are more common. For example, better tests may yield scores in the .75 to .85 range. One common symbol for a reliability value is a lower case italicized letter r with a double x subscript. The double x represents two scores—for example, $r_{xx} = .90$.

Classical Test Theory and Reliability

In classical test theory, an obtained score varies. The variation is called *error*. The theory assumes that a person's true score equals their obtained score plus error. The higher the reliability value, the lower the amount of error. Scores yielding reliability values of .90 have less error than scores producing reliability values of .65.

The reliability values associated with tests will vary depending on the method of testing. I will review a few different methods in the next section.

Test-Retest Reliability

If we give a self-concept scale to a group of people today and again in two days, we can calculate a correlation coefficient for the two sets of scores. In general, we would expect self-concept to be fairly stable over two days thus we would expect a high test-retest correlation coefficient such as $r_{tt} = .88$. The double t in the subscript indicates this reliability coefficient is a test-retest statistic.

You might suspect that time makes a difference. If you take an intelligence test one week after taking it the first time, you might remember some of the problems and figure out the correct answer to the ones you missed. Scores can be higher when retesting intelligence or achievement after a short period of time. Depression can vary a lot more than a factor such as reading ability. Depression can improve or worsen over time. We would not expect scores on a measure of depression to have high retest values over a period of months.

Parallel, Equivalent, and Alternate Forms Reliability

Instead of giving the same test twice, some publishers create two or more forms of a test that are supposed to yield similar scores. Although two sets of test items may be similar, they are not exactly the same, so a perfect correlation will not be possible. Having more than one form can be helpful to overcome problems of retesting with the same items.

Internal Consistency Methods of Reliability

Methods of internal consistency calculate values based on score patterns from one administration of a test. For example, a person with a high degree of anxiety ought to score high on most test items that measure anxiety. Methods of internal consistency are useful because researchers can calculate values based on one administration of a test. Following are two methods to calculate internal consistency.

Split-Half and Odd-Even Reliability

A simple method to calculate internal consistency is to divide a test in half and calculate a correlation coefficient between the scores for the two halves. A common practice is to split the test based on even and odd numbered items.

A problem with this method is that shorter tests generally produce less reliable scores than do longer tests. A mathematical formula can be used to estimate the reliability value for a full set of items based on the value obtained from a split-half calculation. You will see this value referred to in test manuals as *Spearman-Brown*. To use the Spearman-Brown formula, multiply the split-half reliability by 2 and divide by 1 plus the reliability value. For example, if the split-half reliability value for a reading test is .75, we multiply .75 by 2 to get 1.50 then divide 1.50 by 1.75, or (1 + .75), which equals .86 (rounded).

Cronbach's Coefficient Alpha

In counseling research articles, Cronbach's coefficient alpha is a commonly reported internal consistency statistic. This measure is sometimes just referred to as *alpha* or symbolized by the Greek letter α. Alpha represents the average correlation for each pair of items from one administration of a test. Alpha is commonly used with rating scales. For example, in one study, two colleagues and I used items from the Intratextual Fundamentalism Scale to assess fundamentalist beliefs in a sample of Christian counselors. The Cronbach's alpha value was .83 (Sutton, Arnzen, & Kelly, 2016).

Item Response Theory and Reliability

The methods of reliability reported so far are derived from classical test theory. Item Response Theory (IRT) analyzes information about each item in a test to see how well an item functions as a measure of the trait or ability being measured. Item response theory is also known as *latent trait theory*. In presentations, you may just see the acronym IRT. A common example is to look at tests of ability such as intelligence tests. Theoretically, people with high IQ scores should get more items correct than people with low IQ scores. As items increase in difficulty level, people with high intelligence have a better chance at getting more items correct than do people with low intelligence. Researchers can plot the data about each item to see how well the items perform. Each item has a specific pattern. Useful items work well to identify differences in people with low and high ability in the midrange of ability.

Review of reliability

Reliability is a property of test scores, not tests.

The values of a reliability coefficient range from 0.0 to 1.0.

Reliability values can be obtained from different procedures, including the following: test-retest; alternate, equivalent, or parallel forms; and internal consistency methods such as split-half and coefficient alpha.

Item-response theory is a more precise method that looks at the way each item on a test functions in terms of the trait or aptitude being measured.

21. Test Score Validity

What's the purpose of the test?

Objectives:

Define *validity* related to test scores.

Describe common methods of validity.

Test validity addresses the question of purpose. Tests purport to measure something. A test of depression ought to measure depression. There is no single value or method that determines the validity of test scores. Instead, validity is a cumulative concept based on the findings of many studies. As with reliability, our focus is on the scores, not the tests. Recall that scores associated with a test vary every time a test is given. As with reliability, there are different types of validity.

The relationship between reliability and validity can be confusing at first. Here is a common statement: *Reliability is a necessary but not sufficient condition for validity*. Let me unpack that statement. A test may have a history of producing reliable scores—scores that are very stable and have a high degree of internal consistency. However, just because test scores yield reliable findings does not mean the scores will help with a particular purpose. Test scores measuring intelligence in high school may not be valid for predicting success at learning to drive a truck. Test scores from a personality test may not be valid for determining who will be an effective counselor. Test publishers need to state the purpose of their tests and provide evidence of validity based on several studies.

Content Validity

Test developers write test items they believe will assess what the test purports to measure. If we construct a ten-item test to measure introversion each item is a part of the personality trait, which is also called a *construct*. Test developers begin with a definition of a construct like introversion, anxiety, or geometry, and proceed to create items likely to measure attributes of the construct. Experts in a field provide information about the content to be measured. Test items are prepared to match the content. In reality, tests contain items that are samples from an entire subject content called the *test domain*. Content validity is based on the judgment of experts in a given field.

Sometimes face validity is confused with content validity. *Face validity* refers to the appearance of a test from the perspective of a test taker or someone who purchases a test. For example, it might seem odd to have a test of depression that does not ask if a person is sad. Face validity is not a technical aspect of tests. Test scores may have high validity values without appearing valid to a consumer although it might be hard to convince a consumer to take or buy a test that does not look like it measures what it is supposed to measure.

Criterion-Related Validity

Criterion-related validity compares a set of test scores on one test to those from another test using a correlation procedure. A common correlation coefficient is the Pearson r, to which an xy subscript is added to represent scores on two different tests. There are two types of criterion-related validity.

Concurrent validity compares two sets of test scores from a current test study. In one study, some colleagues and I compared a measure of forgiveness with a measure of compassion. We expected a positive correlation because, although the two constructs are not the same, we would question the validity of our measures if they were unrelated or even negatively correlated. It turns out there was a significant positive correlation ($r_{xy} = .25, p < .01$) between the two measures (Sutton, Jordan, & Worthington, 2014).

Another type of criterion-related validity is predictive validity. In this type of validity, a set of test scores is compared to a future criterion. For example, we may wish to see if a measure of high school achievement is a good predictor of GPA at the end of the first year in college.

Construct Validity

Counseling textbooks are full of constructs. Every diagnosis is a construct that includes a list of criteria. When we write about client strengths, we refer to other constructs, such as optimism and hopefulness. *Construct validity* refers to evidence collected using different methods that support the existence of a particular construct, which can be recognized by many independent researchers.

Judgment analysis

If we were to develop a measure of PTSD that may be completed by clients, we would want to know that high scores on the PTSD measure are similar to the diagnoses of PTSD assigned by expert clinicians. If there is a high agreement between the judgment of clinicians and the responses of clients then there is evidence that the test helps measure the construct of PTSD.

Factor Analysis

Factor analysis is a mathematical strategy to analyze groups of items within a large test to see how well they relate to each other. For example, we may expect intelligence to include an understanding of vocabulary and the ability to solve mathematical problems. Our measures of vocabulary and mathematics measure very different constructs, but if they are both aspects of intelligence, we would expect some degree of positive correlation between them and the total test score.

Convergent Validity

Convergent validity can be assessed by comparing two different measures of the same construct. For example, there are several measures of anxiety. If two anxiety tests measure the same construct, the scores ought to result in a significant positive correlation.

Discriminant Validity

Discriminant validity is like the opposite of convergent validity. In convergent validity, we expected to find a positive relationship between two measures of the same or similar constructs. In discriminant validity, we expect to find little or no relationship between dissimilar constructs. We would not expect a measure of courage to be significantly correlated with a measure of visual-spatial ability.

Review of Validity

Validity refers to how well test scores support the purpose of a test.

Validity is a property of test scores, not tests.

High reliability values are important to obtaining high validity values.

Validity, when associated with scores produced by a test, is a broad concept based on the findings from many studies using different methods.

Content validity relies on reports from those with expertise concerning the domain of items a test purports to assess.

Face validity is not a method of determining validity, but it is a term used to describe how valid a test appears to a test taker or purchaser.

Several methods of determining validity produce numerical values. Example methods include: factor analysis, concurrent and predictive validity, convergent and discriminant validity.

Construct validity develops from a collection of evidence from several studies using multiple methods.

Vocabulary

Alpha. The probability of rejecting a true null hypothesis. Alpha also refers to a measure of internal consistency—see Cronbach's coefficient alpha.

Alternate forms reliability. A procedure for obtaining evidence of the reliability of test scores by calculating a reliability coefficient from scores produced by two or more forms of the same test. This is also known as *equivalent forms reliability*. When there are two forms, the term *parallel forms* is sometimes used.

ANOVA. An abbreviation for the statistical procedure known as the *Analysis of Variance*. The procedure analyzes the variance between the means of the groups in a study compared to the variance among the participants in a study. From the resulting ratio, an *F* statistic is calculated.

ANCOVA. Analysis of Covariance is a statistical procedure for analyzing results when there are one or more independent variables, one dependent variable, and one or more covariates.

Categorical variable. Categorical variables are those variables having two or more groups or levels such as sex, ethnicity, and religious group.

Chi-Square. A statistic that can be used to analyze results from categorical variables. The chi-square statistic is used with frequency data.

Coefficient alpha. See *Cronbach's alpha*.

Concurrent validity. A method of test score validity based on the correlation of two sets of scores obtained at the same time.

Confounding variable. A variable that produces unexpected changes in the dependent variable and therefore interferes with interpreting the capacity of an independent variable to produce or explain changes in a dependent variable.

Construct validity. A collection of evidence using different methods that support the existence of a particular construct, which can be recognized by many independent researchers.

Content validity. The extent to which experts judge the items in a test adequately sample the domain a test is supposed to measure.

Continuous variable. A variable having a wide range of numerical values, such as intelligence, achievement, and personality variables.

Correlation. The relationship between two variables. When two variables vary in a specific way with each other, they are said to covary. The covariation can be described in a graph of the relationship or in a summary statistic known as a *correlation coefficient.* There are a few common correlation coefficients.

Correlation coefficient. A statistic that summarizes a correlation between two variables. Correlations range from -1.0 to +1.0. Positive correlation values represent relationships such that as one variable increases, so does the other. Negative correlation values represent relationships that are inverse. In an inverse relationship, one value increases as the other value decreases. A common coefficient is the

Pearson Product Moment Correlation Coefficient reported using a lower case, italicized letter r. See also *correlation*.

Covariate. A variable that is correlated with a dependent variable.

Cramer's V. A correlation coefficient that may be used with nominal data.

Criterion related validity. Criterion-related validity compares a set of test scores on one test to scores on another test using a correlation procedure.

Cronbach's coefficient alpha. A statistic indicating the internal consistency of test items based on an average of the interitem correlations in a sample.

Dependent variable (DV). The variable in a research study that is expected to change when a researcher varies the level of an independent variable.

Degrees of Freedom (*df*). When calculating a statistic, there is a limit on the number of values in a set of data that are free to vary.

Effect size (*ES*). How much of the variance in the dependent variable is accounted for by the independent variable. There are different measures of effect size, such as Cohen's d, r^2, and η^2.

Extraneous variable (EV). A variable in a study that is not supposed to produce a change in a dependent variable. Variations in the temperature and humidity of a testing room are examples of extraneous variables.

F-statistic. The F statistic in this text is the value obtained from an ANOVA procedure. It is also called the F ratio. The letter F is taken from the surname of statistician and biologist, Sir Ronald Fisher.

Face validity. A term used to describe the way a test appears to a test taker or test purchaser. It is not a scientific term for a type of validity and it is sometimes confused with content validity.

Independent variable (IV). The variable in a research study that a researcher manipulates to determine if another variable, the dependent variable, changes when the IV changes.

Item Response Theory (IRT). An analysis of information about each item in a test to see how well an item functions as a measure of the trait or ability being measured.

Kendall's tau. A correlation coefficient that indicates the relationship between sets of ordinal data.

MANOVA (Multivariate Analysis of Variance). A statistical procedure for analyzing results when there are one or more independent variables and two or more dependent variables.

MANCOVA (Multivariate Analysis of Covariance). A statistical procedure for analyzing results when there are one or more independent variables, two or more dependent variables, and one or more covariates.

Mean. The arithmetic average for a set of scores or values.

Median. The number representing the mid-point in a set of scores or values. The median divides a distribution of scores in half. Half the scores are above the median and half the scores are below the median.

Mode. The number representing the most frequent score in a distribution of scores. A distribution may have more than one mode.

Null hypothesis. This is the assumption of no difference between the means stated in terms of population values on the dependent variable. Most researchers only report the research question or research hypothesis and rarely state the null hypothesis. Example: There is no difference between the population means of regular and special education teachers' job satisfaction scores. The statistical null hypothesis is rarely written but is given as $\mu_{:1} = \mu_{:2}$, where Greek letters represent the population means.

Observed Power (*OP*). The probability of finding an effect based on the sample size and effect size.

Parallel forms reliability. See *alternate forms reliability*.

Pearson Product Moment Correlation coefficient. See correlation coefficient.

Population. The entire set of data of interest to a researcher. In counseling research, the population is usually thought of in terms of people who have the characteristics relevant to the topic being studied. For example, if researchers are studying optimism in the elderly, they may define the population of interest as all North Americans above age 70.

Predictive validity. A type of criterion-related validity. A procedure that relies on knowledge about the correlation between two sets of score data to predict future scores or values from the results of a current set of scores or data. For example, predicting future college GPA from knowledge of the relationship between a high school aptitude test and college GPA in previous studies.

Probability (*p*). The probability of falsely rejecting the null hypothesis. The *p* value is commonly compared to an alpha level. Common values include .05, .01, and .001 depending on the nature of the variables and the research questions. Older articles typically reported *p* values as less than or greater than a specified alpha value such as .05. More recent articles report the actual *p* values.

Sample. A small set of data drawn from a large set of data called the population. A population is the entire set of data. In counseling research, data sets are created from the data produced by samples of people drawn from a population.

Spearman's Rank Order Correlation Coefficient. The Spearman Rank Order Correlation Coefficient indicates the relationship between sets of ordinal data.

Standard deviation (*SD*). A statistic based on the deviation of scores from their group mean. The number reveals how much the scores in a distribution deviate from the mean. When the standard deviation is small relative to the mean, the scores are close to the mean, and when the standard deviation is large, the scores are considerably above and below the mean.

Standard Error of Estimate (SEE). A measure of error used to create a range above and below an estimated or predicted value or score. SEE is an indicator of precision in estimating values.

Standard Error of the Mean (SE). A measure of error used to create a range above and below an obtained sample mean suggesting where a mean might fall if means were calculated for repeated samples.

Standard Error of Measurement (SEM). A measure of error used to create a score range above and below an obtained test score suggesting where a person's true score might fall if the test is taken again. SEM is related to the reliability of test scores.

Test reliability. An imprecise but commonly used term about test scores. Tests do not have a specific reliability value because reliability is a product of test scores, which vary with each administration. Reliability values also vary with the method used to obtain the scores in the calculation.

Test-retest reliability. A method of calculating the reliability of test scores based on giving the same test or alternate forms separated by a period of time.

Test validity. Technically, tests do not have a specific validity value because validity is a product of test scores, which vary with each administration. Validity values also vary with the method used to obtain the scores.

Type I error. A Type I error occurs when researchers find their data support their research hypothesis and conclude the null hypothesis is false when in fact the research hypothesis is not supported.

Type II error. A Type II error occurs when researchers conclude their data do not support their research hypothesis. They fail to reject the null hypothesis.

Variable. A characteristic that varies in two or more ways.

Variance (VAR). Variance is the average of the squared differences from the mean of a set of values. The variance of a set of scores is the square of the standard deviation. The variance is a measure of variability used in statistical analyses.

References

Baskin, T. W. & Enright, R. D. (2004). Intervention studies
on forgiveness: A meta-analysis. *Journal of
Counseling & Development, 82,* 79-90.

Cohen, J. (1994). The earth is round (*p* < .05). *American
Psychologist, 49,* 997-1003.

Gosling, S. D., Rentfrow, P. J., & Swann, Jr., W. B. (2003).
A very brief measure of the big-five personality
domains. *Journal of Research in Personality, 37,*
504-528. doi:10.1016/s0092-6566(03)00046-1

NCES (May, 2016). Children and youth with disabilities.
Retrieved from
https://nces.ed.gov/programs/coe/indicator_cgg.asp

Ripley, J. S., Garthe, R. C., Perkins, A., Worthington, E. J.,
Davis, D. E., Hook, J. N., & ... Eaves, D. (2016).
Perceived partner humility predicts subjective stress
during transition to parenthood. *Couple and Family
Psychology: Research and Practice, 5*(3), 157-167.
doi:10.1037/cfp0000063

Snyder, C. R., Harris, C., Anderson, J. R., Holleran, S. A.,
Irving, L. M., Sigmon, S. T., et al. (1991). The will
and the ways: Development and validation of an
individual-differences measure of hope. *Journal of
Personality and Social Psychology, 60,* 570-585.

Styck, K. M., & Walsh, S. M. (2016). Evaluating the prevalence and impact of examiner errors on the Wechsler scales of intelligence: A meta-analysis. *Psychological Assessment, 28*, 3-17. doi:10.1037/pas0000157

Sutton, G. W., Arnzen, C., & Kelly, H. (2016). Christian counseling and psychotherapy: Components of clinician spirituality that predict type of Christian intervention. *Journal of Psychology and Christianity, 35*, 204-214.

Sutton, G.W., & Huberty, T.J. (1984). An evaluation of teacher stress and job satisfaction. *Education, 105*, 189-192.

Sutton, G.W., Koller, J.R., & Christian, B.T. (1982). The Stanford Binet mental age and WISC-R test age: A comparison study. *Psychology in the Schools, 19*, 287-289.

Warner, R. (2013). *Applied statistics: From bivariate through multivariate techniques, 2nd Ed.* Washington, DC: Sage.

Appendix A

The normal curve with percentages indicating the approximate percent of scores falling in the different regions. The numbers beneath the curve are standard deviations.

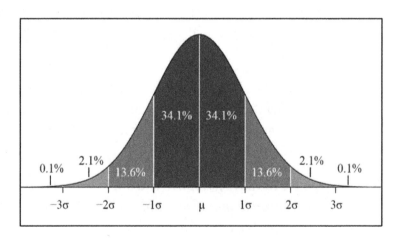

Appendix B

A Table of Values Illustrating Comparable Test Scores

Each row contains the equivalent score on a different scoring system. For example, a z-score of 1 equals a T score of 60, and a standard score of 115. The score is at the 84th percentile.

z	T	Standard	Percentile
3	80	145	99.9
2	70	130	98
1	60	115	84
0	50	100	50
-1	40	85	16
-2	30	70	2
-3	20	55	0.1

Notes

z-scores, $M = 0$, $SD = 1$

T-scores, $M = 50$, $SD = 10$

Standard Scores, $M = 100$, $SD = 15$

Acknowledgements

I am grateful to those who provided feedback on various drafts. Detailed feedback from Nick Schollars was helpful regarding the suitability of the content for those entering a counseling program. Kayla Jordan provided suggestions on the inclusion of additional concepts and other technical matters. Heather Kelly offered suggestions on expanding and clarifying various parts of the text. Dr. Mervin Van der Spuy provided a strong endorsement of this text for all counseling graduate students. Beth Barker provided excellent assistance in editing the final draft.

About the Author

Geoffrey W. Sutton began his professional career as a counselor after obtaining a master's degree in counseling from the University of Missouri-Columbia. He worked in the field of rehabilitation counseling until returning to the University of Missouri for a Ph.D.

He is Emeritus Professor of Psychology of Evangel University in Springfield, Missouri, where he taught courses on assessment, statistics, and research methods in the counseling program. He has more than 100 publications, which include books, book chapters, and articles. His recent interests focus on counseling, spirituality, forgiveness, hope, and compassion.

Connections

Book Website

https://sites.google.com/view/counselorstatistics/

Author Website

www.suttong.com

Author Twitter @GeoffWSutton

https://twitter.com/GeoffWSutton

Author Facebook Page

https://www.facebook.com/Geoff.W.Sutton/

Made in the USA
Coppell, TX
13 January 2022

71529011R00072